The Golden Connection

How Your Relationships Will Make
(or Break) Your Success

Ali Goljahmofrad

© 2016 by Ali Goljahmofrad. All rights reserved. Printed in the United States of America.

No part of this book may be reproduced in any written, electronic, recording, or photocopying without written permission of the author. The exception would be in the case of brief quotations embodied in the critical articles or reviews and pages where permission is specifically granted by the author.

Some names have been changed to protect the privacy of individuals.

Additional books can be purchased on Amazon.com or through the author's website: www.aligoljahmofrad.com.

For bulk sale discounts, information, and other inquiries, email alig@aligoljahmofrad.com.

10 9 8 7 6 5 4 3 2 1

Dedicated to my mother, Maryanne, and to my father, Kamran, for giving me an upbringing that few children get to enjoy.

To my sister, Natasha, and my brothers, Auriya and Armon, for constantly challenging me and making me a better person.

To my wife, Marilee, for being an unwavering support in *every single* thing I do.

To my friends, all of whom I consider family.

And finally, to you reading this right now. I wrote this for you.

Acknowledgments

Sir Isaac Newton is famously quoted as claiming, "If I have seen further, it is by standing on the shoulders of giants." I am by no means comparing myself to one of the greatest minds of all time, but I can relate to what he is saying.

The fact that you're holding this book in your hands right now is a testament to this point. In it, you are going to read about very personal lessons that all came about because of the help and love from others. In addition to this, the actual process of making this book a reality wouldn't have happened without the assistance from many people.

I may have had two of the best, most thorough editors an author could ask for. Jessica Hoffman-Ramirez and LeAnne Schultz found a healthy balance of tearing my work to shreds while simultaneously giving me a few attaboys. In addition to the content, the cover and layout wouldn't have been possible without the help of Paul Schultz, Carina Jones, and Allison Boerger. I never knew that simply trying to add a header and footer could be so frustrating!

In addition to the logistical assistance these four incredible people provided, the support from those around me proved to be critical in completing this book. Of all the support I received, none was as motivating and useful as the patience and understanding I got from my wife. After long school days of not seeing each other, I'd have to write to keep up with my publication schedule. Wanting to spend time with each other, we knew a goal was set, and she supported me in hitting it.

Sometimes this meant not seeing each other until it was time for bed. It simply can't be overstated how much her support pushed me.

Just know this, I'm surrounded by giants.

Table of Contents

Dedication v

Acknowledgments vii

Foreword xiii

Introduction xvii

Ch 1 That One Jump 1

Ch 2 A Suicide Attempt 7

Ch 3 Governors and Multipliers 15

Ch 4 When You Give, You Receive 21

Ch 5 Work On You 29

Ch 6 A Church Mission Call 35

Ch 7 Jack Johnson Made Me Do It 41

Ch 8 We're Friends Because 49

Ch 9 Beth 57

Ch 10 Sylvester Stallone Got Me Paid 65

Ch 11 A Fraud and a Check 71

Ch 12 Respect Your Elders Is Dead 79

Ch 13 Dialogue Is Everything 85

Ch 14 Theory of Resources 89

Ch 15 Inside The Box 97

Ch 16 Quitting To Start 103

Ch 17 You Can't Stay Dry In A Pool 111

Ch 18 The Journey 119

Yesterday I was clever, so I wanted to change the world. Today I am wise, so I am changing myself.

-Rumi

Foreword

Writing a book is easy.

But writing a book truly worth reading is a crucible. From its opening pages to its powerful conclusion, it is clear that author Ali Goljahmofrad has invested heavily over every word of *The Golden Connection*. Accordingly, his debut book proves to be a book truly worth reading.

But let me explain why.

I've discovered that of all the factors that go in to writing a book worth reading—knowledge of the subject matter, experience, patience, etc.—there's another characteristic that overshadows them all. That is—courage. No author ever wrote a successful book without courage. This is because in addition to the aforementioned factors that are most relevant prior to publication, courage also requires the author to have foresight into the book's impact after publication.

The author must have the courage to lay his life bare, expose his flaws, accept his weaknesses, and trust the readership to accept him for who he is. But beyond that, the courageous author must show with clarity that his success is not in spite of his flaws—but because of them.

I reflected over this as I read *The Golden Connection*. And having done so, I can only conclude that it is one of the most courageous books I've ever had the pleasure of reading. Ali has presented a narrative that few authors have the courage to write. While all too often motivational books focus on mere theory or the hypothetical struggles of someone else, Ali delves in head first by laying bare some of the most real, raw, and intimate struggles of his life.

And in doing so, he not only becomes incredibly relatable, but he does something more. Rather than simply inviting the reader to trust him, Ali earns that trust with genuine narratives of courage, compassion—and yes even by relating his failures. This courage and authenticity permeates each page of *The Golden Connection*, and leaves you turning the pages without a break.

Far from some boring academic read, Ali harnesses the truly awesome power of storytelling with humor, suspense, and engaging dialogue. Whether it's the horrifying story about a family member who attempted suicide, the life altering story of overcoming losing one's faith, or the inspiring story of understanding that true love is a reality—if we choose for it to be—the narratives he illustrates grab you by your heart and spark a brainstorm of activity.

Ali and I met through the magic of social media some time ago. And in our conversations and in person meetings since, I've been fortunate to see an inspiring young man incessantly embrace the courageous mission to serve others with every fiber of his being. He speaks from a position of humility, wisdom, and honesty, making his voice all the more attractive. Ali will accomplish a great many more things in his life. Many years from now people will look back and point to *The Golden Connection* as his launch pad—so it's good you're getting in now.

If you're seeking a preachy book that sugarcoats life, look elsewhere. But if you're seeking an inspiring read that addresses the harsh realities of life and offers inspiring perspectives, I have no doubt you will find immense value in this book. So, as you pick up *The Golden Connection*, hold on tight.

You're in for a courageous journey.

Qasim Rashid, Esq.
Author of *Talk to Me: Changing the Narrative on Race, Religion, & Education*
Harvard University Fellow 2015-16
National Spokesperson Ahmadiyya Muslim Community USA

Introduction

One day during the fall of 2015, my cell phone rang. **Dad Cell** appeared on the screen. "Hey, how's it going?" I asked, without saying hello.

"Oh not too bad, just calling to see how you're doing. What are you up to?"

"I'm reading *How to Win Friends and Influence People*." I'd recommend it.

"Reading that book? You should be *writing* that book." I don't think my dad actually realized how much credit he was trying to give me, but it was a moment that made me really start to think.

This book has been a process, specifically a 30 year process. I believe I have had a life of unique fortune and incredible relationships. It is because of my relationships that I made it out of high school in one piece, somehow navigated my way through college, and find myself in a place of satisfaction with who I am. All of this, because of relationships.

In the following pages you will read some of my own personal stories, and stories from others, that are littered with lessons that weren't always the easiest to learn, but added to the understanding of how our associations with those around us work and benefit us.

This is not an exhaustive list of what we must do to find success. This is not an exhaustive list of how to make all of our relationships work. This is collection of practical ideas that you can use in your everyday life to hopefully make you a better person today than you were yesterday.

This book is not just for teenagers, and it's certainly not just for adults. This book is for the person who is courageous enough to look in the mirror and ask, "Is there anything I can do today that will make me a better person for those around me?" When it's all said and done, it's the way you impacted others that will matter.

Before we begin, know that I think you're incredible.

You're somebody who matters.
You're somebody this world desperately needs.
You're somebody *somebody* needs.

1
That One Jump

If you're going to risk and fail, fail at something that matters. Fail gloriously so that even in failure, lives change.
— Jon Acuff

The weather could not have been more perfect, a comfortable 75 degrees. The afternoon sun was giving just the right amount of warmth, blue skies with sporadic fluffy white clouds, and a consistent breeze so slight that you might not notice it unless you were paying attention. Summertime in Southeast Idaho is perfect.

I was riding my BMX bike with one of my best friends in front of my house. I lived in a subdivision that was established, but builders had recently started expanding the neighborhood into some undeveloped land, so we had a giant field of dirt hills right across the street. We would go out into the field and add to certain hills to build small jumps. We tried to make our own little trails in what was our best attempt to be extreme BMX'ers.

We failed.

I remember getting so frustrated with my friend John because he could ride the jumps and trails so flawlessly, effortlessly. It was as if he didn't really have to try. Then I'd come along over-thinking and under-peddling my way to embarrassment. I remember one jump in particular that was actually three smaller jumps, one right after the other. If you hit the first one fast enough it would shoot you over the second, landing you softly on the third.

John hit the jump time and time again, easily clearing the middle mound, and would then invite me to try the same. I was scared though. I would never build up enough speed to hit the first jump hard enough. I would peddle hard, anticipate the flight path, and focus on the ramp, but right as I would get to the jump, I would chicken out and hit the brakes. I would shamefully roll over all three hills, much like a bowling ball does at the Bowler Roller carnival game. You know, that one that was impossible to make the bowling ball stay at the end of the track? I can't stand that game. It has false hope written all over it! Just as the bowling ball would hit the end and bounce back, I would turn my bike around and tell myself, "Okay, *this* time for real." Ha, yeah right. No matter how much I tried to lie to myself, I was not brave when it came to anything remotely dangerous.

John would always assure me that I could do it. He said I had the speed, the path, and that I was just missing the follow through. He showed me a couple of more times, which built up my confidence, and then he told me it was my turn. After some reluctance, John's encouragement turned to frustration and he started letting me know what he really thought of my hesitation. To this day, he is one of my best friends, and best friends don't hold their tongues when criticizing each other. Needless to say, John wasn't being the nurturing coach that he had been before.

I consider myself a competitor, so I took the words as fuel and started that good ol' positive self-talk. "*Okay, I've got this. I have the speed, I have the path. John said it himself, and he's done this before, so I'm good. Stop being scared. If he can do it, you can do it.*" Off I peddled. I peddled hard, I peddled fast. I thought of reasons I *should* follow through. This is a small obstacle that would only build my confidence even more. This was an opportunity to look fear in the face and say, "I'm bigger than you!"

I approached the jump with plenty of speed, passed the point where I usually tapped my brakes, and realized I wasn't dead yet. I kept going and hit the jump with more speed than before, pulled up on my handlebars, and then realized I should've let the jump do the work. My front tire was *not* in the same position John's was every time he jumped, so I pushed down on the handlebars with as much force as I needed to get the bike level again. Here is where I should let you know about one tiny detail. Right before I left the jump, I ever-so-slightly tapped my brakes. Just a hair. Like, it wasn't even noticeable to anybody else, but I did not go into that jump with as much speed as I needed. So here I was in the middle of the air, trying to push my front tire down, and I didn't have enough speed.

My front tire slammed into the jump just underneath the lip of the take-off and that shot me forward and down to the ground where the left side of my forehead broke my fall, my body compressing like a fleshy accordion on the ground. Head, neck, back, and legs all tried to gather as the bike followed and was the disgraceful cherry on top of my worst attempt yet. It hurt physically, but the emotional pain was way worse.

You see, the problems we face in our respective lives are not too different than me trying to complete this jump. We have the necessary information, equipment, coaching, support, and desire, but our actual attempts are where we fall short, sometimes literally. We fall short for many different reasons. Maybe we're too scared (like I was), maybe we want more answers before starting, or maybe we simply aren't prepared enough. In my case, with this jump, I had what I needed, but I tapped the brakes *just enough* to stop me from reaching my goal. Why did I hit the brakes? Easy, fear. I was scared of the unknown. I kept asking myself: *"What if I fall short? What if I go too fast? What if I'm off center?"* I kept asking all these questions in my mind that were related to failure. I am reminded of this short poem from Erin Hanson:

> *"There is freedom waiting for you, on the breezes of the sky. And you ask, "What if I fall?" Oh, but my darling, what if you fly?"*

I was too focused on what could go wrong with the jump instead of what could go right. Denis Waitley said that our minds dictate our bodies to move towards our currently dominant thought. So for Olympians, they don't tell themselves, *"Don't fall, don't slip, don't lose."* Olympians tell themselves, *"You have good balance, you've succeeded here before, win."* It is a small shift in thinking that makes a world of difference.

This feeling is all too familiar with people today. Feelings of fear, inferiority, and the idea that we are not necessarily equipped with the proper skill set keeps us from "attempting the jump." What ideas are you hanging on to that prohibit you from thinking you're capable? What are you telling yourself that is talking you out of moving forward?

Let me suggest that I *know* you already have what it takes to reach your goals. I know it because if you're bold enough to imagine the possibilities, you're gifted enough to reach them. I'm not going to be the one to say it won't hurt. It will. Like trying to tackle the jump, sometimes pain is a part of the process. But no amount of pain will last compared to the satisfaction of knowing you kept trying.

Key Takeaways from Chapter 1

1- Nobody is going to jump for you. If *you* want something, go get it. Nobody else is in charge of *your* goals.

2- Even when it seems like you have all the necessary information, you might fall short, and it's going to be uncomfortable. But you can't give up because it didn't go as planned.

3- When trying to do something you're afraid of, having the right company won't make the problem go away, but having the right company might give you the belief that you can do it.

There are many principles I take away from the bike experience, and we will cover some of them later on. But first, I want to talk about the day an ambulance raced down my street and why it turned out to be one of the best days of my life.

2
A Suicide Attempt: One of the Best Days of My Life

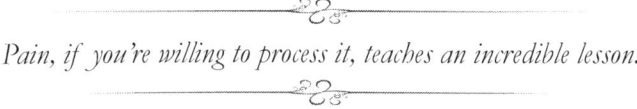

Pain, if you're willing to process it, teaches an incredible lesson.

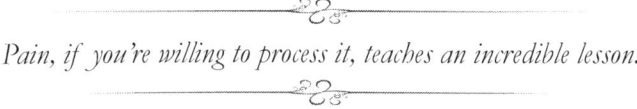

I grew up in a small town called Rigby. It had a hair under 3,000 people when I was growing up, and barely broke that mark when I graduated high school. In my opinion, it is a perfect little town. It had everything we needed to have fun, and just enough to get into trouble every now and then.

In Rigby, it seems like everybody knows each other. It is literally impossible to go to Broulim's, the local grocery store, without seeing somebody you know. Rigby is a tight-knit community as well. High school athletics are heavily supported, religious activities are regularly attended, and most people were involved in one, if not both of those. I cannot emphasize enough how small of a town Rigby is. Two stop lights were all we ever had to wait at in high school. There is no such thing as rush hour

The Golden Connection

traffic, although every now and then you will get stuck behind a tractor. Usually you only encounter a tractor if you venture beyond the 2 square miles of the "city."

Rigby was built in the middle of a classic country grid that ran North-South and East-West. We lived on the Northwest edge of town, sitting behind my elementary school. Not much happened in Rigby, let alone any of its neighborhoods. Generally, crimes ranged from me and my friends doorbell ditching our neighbors to toilet-papering a house. Real gangster stuff.

Like many beautiful days when I was 15, I found myself in front of my house riding my bike. I was still trying to build up the courage that never came to attack that god-forsaken jump. But, there we were, just some friends enjoying the beautiful Idaho weather while it lasted. Then all of sudden, off in the distance, I heard a siren. No big deal, it wasn't *completely* out of the ordinary to hear a siren, but I did notice it. We continued to ride, minding our own business. Maybe a minute or two passed and I realized that not only were the sirens not going away, they were getting closer.

I waited as the sirens grew louder, realizing that the sound was definitely headed our way. Our neighborhood was situated in a way that there was one way in and one way out. If the sirens were close enough to hear that clearly, they were in my neighborhood. Now, in Rigby, it can't be said that *everybody* knows *everybody*, but practically. And as for my neighborhood, everybody *did* know everybody.

Before I knew it, an ambulance turned down 4th North. My street, Marian Court, connected at the end of 4th North. I thought, *No way. It doesn't matter where this ambulance stops, I know every family on this block*. You could point to a house and anybody

8

from our neighborhood could tell you who lived there, by name. I immediately started to consider who the oldest households were. *Them, no. Them, no. They're not that young. Maybe it's them.* I shuffled through the houses anticipating where the ambulance might stop. It didn't. It kept driving down 4th North toward Marian Court.

My street had three houses on it: the superintendent and his wife, my house, and the Pickett's, our close family friends. When the ambulance reached the end of 4th North, my heart started to beat even faster. It didn't matter if it turned right or left, again, I knew every family on the street. So I really wanted the ambulance to turn around and drive away. Well, it didn't. It turned right and stopped directly in front of my house.

Without hesitation, I started peddling and shot toward my house. My mind was the only thing racing faster than my bike. In this moment there was one thing I didn't know and there was one thing I did know. The one thing I didn't know was what exactly was going on inside the house. The one thing I did know was that my mom was alone when I left to go ride.

As soon as I reached the yard I jumped off my bike and let it ghost ride to a crashing stop as I sprinted inside. On the main level there was nothing, nobody. I heard commotion upstairs and quickly headed that way. I ran up the stairs, turned right into my mom's bedroom, and saw her lying on her bed. She was surrounded by paramedics who were checking her vitals, giving her oxygen, and asking her a lot of questions. I don't vividly remember everything in this moment, but I remember what I felt.

The Golden Connection

My mom and dad got divorced when I was three years old. I've seen seven divorces between the two of them. Jerry was my first step-dad. Growing up, I didn't like Jerry, and he didn't really like me. But we both loved my mom, so it sort of had to work. Jerry was a functioning alcoholic: he was a hard worker, cussed like the worst sailor you'd ever met, and was as rough around the edges as you would expect an alcoholic to be. He was skinny, but strong, and had a few tattoos that looked like he had done himself (if I am not mistaken, the joint of marijuana on his forearm actually was self-issued during his military days).

Jerry was a simple guy. He was a boiler mechanic and loved to work on things. He had a neatly kempt garage with each tool in its rightful place, and God be with you if you ever used something without his permission. Jerry would spend a majority of his nights hanging out in the garage drinking countless cans of Natural Ice beer and smoking cheap cigarettes that he would tear the filter off of.

Though we didn't see eye-to-eye on hardly anything, Jerry provided for us. He worked hard and kept a steady income. We all have our own battles, and alcoholism was one of his. I remember many alcohol-induced arguments between him and my mom as she tried to reason with an inebriated mind.

One evening, I remember being told to pack my bags because we (my mom, sister, and me) were going somewhere else for the night. Eventually, things would settle down and we would end up staying, but it was a roller-coaster at times. Sober Jerry was actually a very nice guy, but drunk Jerry was something else. Though I don't think I ever admitted this to anybody, drunk Jerry scared me.

My mom and Jerry were married for 13 years. Sick of the alcohol and fights, my mom had had enough. They filed for divorce. In addition to the typical struggles of divorce, the timing of it all amplified the problem. My mom lost her father in 1996, her mother in 1999, and my sister had just gone off to college. Never having gotten over my grandmothers death, my mom struggled with depression. Combine all of that, the divorce process with Jerry, financial struggles, and my mom admittedly was in a very bad place.

Feeling like her problems were greater than her ability to solve them, she ingested a bottle of pills in hopes to wipe away the pain. The thing is, pain never truly goes away, it simply gets transferred to another place. How we deal with our pain is different from person to person, but there is no doubt a healthy and unhealthy way to deal with it.

Staring at my mom overdosing on her bed and surrounded by paramedics was an intense experience as a teenager. It would have been for anybody. I felt alone. I felt betrayed. I felt angry. Here I was a high school kid who had a good relationship with his mom, a relationship that was always very comfortable, stable, and warm. It was a relationship I knew I could rely on, but this moment tested that.

I remember thinking *What the hell are you doing?* I remember feeling so angry that she would make that decision. My dad had moved to Arizona for work, my sister was five hours away, I couldn't stand my step-dad, and I had just witnessed my mom attempting suicide. 'Angry teenager' perfectly describes the mindset I was in.

In this moment, though, I learned a few lessons. I learned that great people make great mistakes. No matter who you are, no matter what you've accomplished, no matter what your past is, we all make mistakes. And we all make *big* mistakes. This was a massive mistake made by my incredible mom. She had a reason as to why she chose to do that, but it didn't justify her actions. With that said, and you cannot miss this part: **our mistakes do not define us, how we respond to our mistakes does**!

We are not defined by a single event. My mom almost took her own life, some people fall back into addiction, and some go back on their word to their family, but those events do not define us. Have you ever felt like you made a decision that was irreversible? Mistakes, big and small, are a part of life. I am not excusing them, and I am not condoning them. However, it is necessary to understand that they are normal. One event doesn't write your legacy.

We are defined by either the slow and steady decay we call failure, or by the gradual climb we call progress. Both of which are dictated by our choices *over time*.

The second lesson I learned is that everybody battles something. The person you look up to and the person you look down on are fighting a battle, even if you don't see it. I was an oblivious teenager that could never have predicted how that day would go, but it happened. And it happened because all human beings are fighting a battle. Sometimes our battles are small, easy to overcome. Sometimes our battles seem so daunting all we want to do is sleep, cry, or both. One thing is for sure, if you are living, you will always be fighting for something. That's not a bad thing, that's simply Life happening.

The third lesson I learned from my mom's suicide attempt is the value of relationships. I said that I felt alone that day. I felt like if my mom was willing to leave me behind, who *wouldn't?* I didn't immediately realize how difficult the following months and the next couple of years would be. The slippery slope of seeing a struggling parent is real. I had nights I wouldn't wish upon anybody. I had nights when I'd lie in bed and think, *If I were to kill myself, would I put the gun in my mouth, or to my head? Would I really use a gun? Where would I do it? Who would find me?* I don't share this to make you cringe, I share this because I need you to realize that my relationships saved me from a potentially very dark place.

But I didn't realize this immediately. I didn't see right away that as I was about to fall, I was surrounded by an army of family, friends, and loved ones who recognized the situation and jumped to action. It took time. No words will ever be written that adequately cover, identify, and thank everybody for the role they played in this situation. But because of how the following years played out, I was taught an important lesson about relationships: they are the key to a happy life. Even if your life isn't perfect.

Not too long ago, I gave a speech titled "One of the Best Days of My Life." I went on to tell the story about my mom's suicide attempt. Naturally, the audience was a bit confused. I can still hear their minds, "*How could this possibly be one of the best days of his life?*" This day gave me these three gifts that I will carry with me forever. First, it helped me with my perspective regarding individual struggle, relationships, and how to overcome problems. Second, it helped me identify the true definition of 'family.' Finally, it helped me realize that no matter what happens, we are *never* alone. That is why I say it is one of the best days of my life.

I did not immediately realize how valuable this day would become to me. In the moment, I hardly appreciated it. That's how most lessons progress. When things aren't going right, we tend to not see what we're about to learn from it. It's not easy, it's not fun, and it's not painless. But sure enough, as time goes on, things seem to work themselves out.

One cannot live a poor life if they have rich relationships. Conversely, one cannot live a rich life with poor relationships. Relationships are truly the secret to success. No greater investment can be made than the investment you make in yourself and your relationships.

Key Takeaways from Chapter 2

1- It doesn't matter what people look like. Jerry wasn't always easy to deal with (but neither was I). But just because he wasn't easy to be around doesn't mean he didn't put food on our table and a roof over our heads. We all have shortcomings, but we all add value.

2- Great people make great mistakes. We can't let that define them.

3- We all have hurdles to jump over. Some are taller than others, but nobody's lane is completely clear.

I share the story about my mother with her permission, of course, and I do so because of the lesson it taught me regarding relationships. That's what this book is all about, our relationships. Actually, that's what *life* is all about.

3
Governors and Multipliers

Don't let other people hold you back to make them feel comfortable about doing nothing.
— Stephen Luke

In each of our lives we all experience moments that we would consider pivotal to who we are today. I think of it much like a math equation. Now, don't close the book, I am not turning this into a math lesson. I am simply suggesting that our life experiences can be compared to numbers and operations.

Sometimes we have wonderful, exhilarating, uplifting experiences that multiply and add to our joy, and sometimes life aggressively takes away and divides. For example, up to this point, your life has thrown you a lot of experiences. Hopefully a lot of positives, and undoubtedly your fair share of negatives.

The Golden Connection

Think of these experiences as an equation like this one:

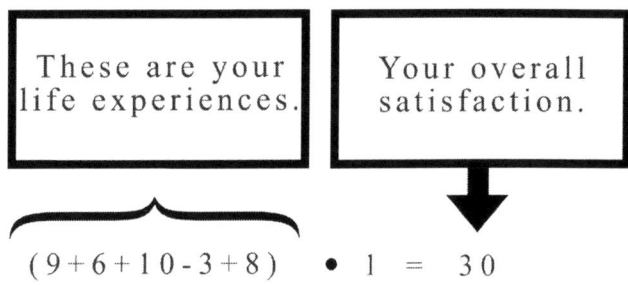

$(9 + 6 + 10 - 3 + 8) \bullet 1 = 30$

The longer you've been alive, the longer your equation is. The sum total of your life is dictated by *what* you experience and *who* you experience it with. So there are two factors to your overall satisfaction.

First, experiences have value. If you do something that adds to your life, and you do it alone, your experience is what it is. Nothing more, nothing less. But if you have company during the experience, your company can amplify or diminish the overall satisfaction. That is the second factor, the company you keep.

We have all been somewhere thinking *man, this is great, except for the fact that* this *person is here*. So the sum of your life is your level of satisfaction with your experiences up to this very point. You can have an amazing plan of things to do and places to go, but if you don't have the right relationships in order, then an experience that was supposed to be a 10 is taken down a few notches, or in the worst case, turned into a negative.

Think of this like a governor on a vehicle. Vehicles today are built with these limiters in place to stop people from driving over a certain speed. You can have the sweetest car, with a racing package, the upgraded suspension, and all the other bells and whistles. But, with this device on the car, it doesn't matter how much horse power it claims, what size the engine is, or what transmission it has, you cannot go faster than the governor will allow.

The problem I see in people's lives is that they are involved in relationships that are a governor to their happiness, their success, and their peace of mind. I am not merely talking about a relationship with a spouse, boyfriend, or girlfriend. I am talking about *all* relationships. Some people have everything they need to be happy, except the right relationships.

Now, consider the same equation as before. Life is the sum of positive and negative experiences. Let's assume now we take those same experiences and the only thing we change are the relationships we had through them. Think of the relationship as a multiplier at the end of the equation.

I am going to call a multiplier that is less than one a "governor" because that is limiting our overall sum. I am going to call a multiplier that is at least one a "turbo," as that boosts our overall experience.

<u>Life with the **wrong** relationships will have a **governor**</u>
$$(9 + 6 + 10 - 3 + 8) \,\mathbf{(.5)} = 15$$

<u>Life with the **right** relationships will have a **turbo**</u>
$$(9 + 6 + 10 - 3 + 8) \,\mathbf{(1.5)} = 45$$

You can take two people, give them *literally* the same sequence of experiences, but have two completely different outcomes because of that multiplier. The person who has focused on maintaining the proper relationships will have a much higher level of satisfaction than the one who doesn't ensure quality connections. Relationships are critical to our happiness and are either fertilizer to our success, or the fuel to the fire the burns us. Therefore, it is *vital* that we are actively engaged in doing everything we can to build healthy relationships.

So what does that mean? What does it mean to be "actively engaged" in doing what we can for our relationships? Here's what it means: We must be meticulous in our considerations and deliberate in our actions. Let me explain:

My wife and I have a few policies we try to stick to in our relationship. For example, we have a policy that states we cannot walk into our house on the phone after we haven't seen each other all day. This seems simple, but the effect it has is very real.

I had never considered how it made my wife feel when I would leave early in the morning for school, be gone all day, then walk in talking on the phone when I got home. Maybe I had missed a call during the day or I might have called a friend just to catch up, but I wouldn't think twice about walking in the door after school, deep in a conversation. Looking back, I am a little embarrassed at how negligent I was, but I am fortunate enough to be married to somebody who is willing to discuss issues with me.

She brought up how me doing this made her feel. She pointed out that she understood that some phone calls are necessary, but asked me to finish them before I walked in our home. It's a small change, a simple change, but I can tell you that being greeted with a hug and a kiss is way healthier for a relationship than two raised eyebrows that say "I'll be off the phone shortly."

It takes a little more effort to be deliberate with our actions, but the payoff can be great. In the case of our phone call policy, I've had to deliberately say, "Well, I'm just getting home and I don't walk into the house on the phone. So I'll talk to you later." I had to thoughtfully consider how this affected the two of us. And I continually have to be deliberate about ending my phone calls sooner.

This is a very simple example of what I mean by being considerate and deliberate. If you are to continue to grow the relationship, you must be willing to consider what it needs and then meticulously care for it. That's why anybody who has ever had a successful relationship with a spouse, coworker, or peer will tell you that relationships require work.

I cannot overstate the importance of relationships. As I mentioned earlier, it is my relationships that have seen me through the most difficult times of my life. When a parent attempts suicide, it is hard for the child to not wonder if that could possibly be the answer to difficulty. I now know that suicide is *never* the answer, but arriving at that conclusion was a process aided by those around me.

I shiver at the idea of *what if I didn't have the right relationships through these times?* Well, I did. And I learned from them.

Key Takeaways from Chapter 3

1- Our life experiences can be improved or held back because of our relationships.

2- It is necessary to work to provide a healthy environment for our relationships to grow.

I am not sure if the average person focuses so much on relationships, but I don't believe that you are average. I believe that anybody who is willing to pick up a book and read is special. Furthermore, I believe that anybody who is willing to read a book like this one is extra special. Too many people think they have it all figured out, when in reality we are all trying to figure it out one day at a time. Let me take this opportunity to say thank you for being somebody who is willing to work on yourself.

Now, we just covered why relationships are so important. But how do they actually benefit us? To answer that, I have to share a few very special people with you, people who helped me realize that giving up is not an option.

4
When You Give, You Receive

No one is useless in this world who lightens the burdens of another.
– Charles Dickens

As I think back to all the people who helped me along the way, the list is staggering. It is often said that it takes a village to raise a child. Well, in my case, I'd argue that a few villages pooled their resources together, and I am grateful for those "villages."

It is only fitting that I write this book with the help and input of others. I got jobs with the help of others, I graduated high school with the help of others, I set goals with the help of others, I finished college with the help of others, and I am where I am today with the help of others. My story, lessons, and successes all have been influenced by others, so I wanted some of the "others" to share a little bit.

In everybody's game of life, there are always a few key players. I got a hold of a couple of mine to ask two very simple questions:

Why did you help me? How did you benefit from helping me?

I share these special stories with you because they came at a very crucial time for me. Between the ages of 14 and 19, I was not an easy person to deal with. It was the relationships that I was fortunate to have that pulled me through a lot of adversity, a lot of which was brought on by my own poor choices.

These are a few of many incredible people who were involved in another human's life when they didn't have to be. There were countless people who helped me out during that time. I could write volumes if I expounded on everybody.

I don't have to rack my brain to know how *I* benefited from people intervening, but I wanted to know what *they* got out of it. Why would somebody step in and help a teenager who wasn't theirs? It is critical to realize that relationships are always a two-way street. The people I messaged are a few of many that I owe more than I'll ever be able to repay. The first person I contacted was a police officer from my hometown. Officer Mike was a man I have always looked up to. For seemingly no apparent reason, he was always so supportive. He was actually the catalyst for one of my most unique life experiences that involved Herman Boone, the man who the film *Remember the Titans* was made after. Here is his response to my questions and how he remembers giving me the visit of a lifetime:

> *After teaching thousands of DARE (Drug Abuse Resistance Education) students over the past 24 years, you can see a lot of traits in the kids you teach of where they may likely head. Unfortunately, some of them pick paths that seem to lead to destruction and a life of unhappiness. I have seen some of them that didn't look like they had much of a bright future due to current circumstances make quite a contribution to society, because of the right mentoring. And, I have also seen some who*

seemed to have all of the opportunities for higher education, good family support, etc. that have made decisions that have been very detrimental.

I have come to realize that every person has their own abilities to choose the path they are on. No one can make that decision for them, but others can greatly influence them in the decisions they make. One thing that I have seen that contributes to the success of others is that when someone has somebody in their life that truly believes in them and cares for them, they will do what they can to succeed and make them proud.

I remember teaching you in DARE. You were a great kid and were just great to be around. After you graduated from DARE, I didn't see you around a lot, but would see you every now and then. One night I was working late for some reason and I was out of my normal routine for work. Earlier in the day I remember praying and asking God for an opportunity to be at the right place, at the right time, to make a difference in someone's life. It was late, and as I was driving down the street, I ran across two young men who I taught a few years earlier. One of them was you.

We spoke and I challenged you to be good. And, I felt like I needed to step it up on being involved in your life more than I had been up to that point. As I left, I found myself worried about you. There was nothing you said, it was just a feeling that I had. I remember thinking that God had answered a prayer for me, and that I had just been at the right place at the right time.

The night I ran into you was during the summer of 2001. Later that year, in December, I had a DARE graduation coming up. I had Coach Herman Boone coming to speak for the DARE graduation. While here, he would have some time to help me do some good in the community. I thought back to the visit I had with you that one late night on the streets. I remember we talked about your love for football. I remember thinking how sad it was that you loved football that much and that your father was unable to come watch you play your games and cheer for you, due to being out of state; I think that is important that kids have their parents involved in their lives to cheer them on. I told Coach Boone about you, your love of football, and asked if he would be willing to go make a surprise visit to you. He very willingly accepted the idea.

The look on your face when you realized that Coach Herman Boone was standing in your living room was something I will never forget.

To be honest, there was something in it for me. I was hoping that by me arranging for a celebrity, who loves football and had a movie made about him, who was willing to come visit you in small-town Idaho, you would have no doubt that there were people who thought the world of you and really cared about where you went in life.

What this experience helped me understand is that when people realize that someone truly cares about where they are going in life, they will try to succeed to make them proud. I see so many kids today that are criticized by their parents or peers in about everything they do and it kills me. All people want is to know that someone loves them and sees potential in them. I know all people need to be disciplined at times, and that is ok, but discipline can be done with love and care. I have learned that people will become exactly what we expect and believe them to be.

In my career, when helping people, there has been no greater benefit than to look for the good in others, and let them know what I see in them. I have learned that we have got to love people unconditionally, with no strings attached. People do mess up, that is part of life, but people can also improve. Coming to this understanding is how I benefited from helping you.

When You Give, You Receive

Mike is in that category of relationships that will always be strong. Do you have those connections with people where you might not talk for a year, but then one day you pick up the phone and it is like you haven't skipped a beat? That's my relationship with Mike. He is somebody I consider family. When I received that response from him, it was a relief in a way. I knew he had helped me, but I wondered if he felt like he got anything from his efforts. It is safe to say he did.

The second person I messaged was a family friend named Krista. She, her husband Bryan, and their five kids allowed me a place in their home during my senior year of high school. My mom and I had moved to a different city to find cheaper housing and it was great for the financial aspect, but added a 25-30 minute commute from our apartment to the school each morning. Also, I had recently gotten myself into some legal trouble via a prank gone wrong. Well, I was the only one who found the joke funny (it wasn't funny, it was stupid), and it got me kicked out of high school with all of my friends, and thrown into alternative high school. So Krista and her family stepped in to help.

Their family lived in my hometown, so my commute was substantially easier. My time in their home taught me a lot about family. They don't know this, but their self-proclaimed chaotic house was actually quite comforting to me. They seamlessly accepted me into their home, held me to the same expectations, and helped where they could. This taught me that "family" has nothing to do with blood. Blood defines relation. Love defines family. Krista gave me this response to my questions:

> *We benefited in so many ways. First and foremost is that you truly became a part of our family. I believe that people come into our lives for so many different reasons, some are immediately apparent, and some we may not always know until much later in life. My kids all really came to love you and think of you as a*

The Golden Connection

sibling, and we all really grew to love you. I think of a situation when you got after our daughter over something, and not just any of Rhett's friends (Rhett is their son, we are the same age) would have gotten away with it, but I think she actually appreciated the fact that you cared about her as a little sister.

I also think we all learned to appreciate the things we had been blessed with. Although we were not a family of means, what we had, we could share. The respect you showed both Bryan and I set an example that we weren't completely out of touch in what we expected from our own kids. I believe that our own kids learned not to take for granted little things that we had or did as a family. Obviously we all learned and were reminded that there are unexpected consequences from bad choices, and we usually have very little control over what they are. But, if we do our part, hopefully we can recover from them.

One particular thing that you said to me that I have thought about many times was on a Sunday morning when we were going through our usual chaos and rush to get ready for church. You asked me why we bothered to do this every Sunday. With six kids of my own, this had become somewhat of a routine that I really didn't think about that much. Your question made me stop and think, it would be so much easier to just stay home from church. Not only was it a hassle to get ready, but sitting through our meetings could sometimes look like a circus act, and feel like a disaster. The only answer I had for you at the time was that it is just what we do. I'm not certain that we had ever made a conscious decision about it, but for me personally, I had not grown up with all of my family attending church together, and it was something that I always wanted. We are far, far, far from perfect, but I wanted my children to know that it truly mattered to me. So that helped me find an answer to your difficult question.

Again, knowing that they too felt like they benefited from the relationship is a relief. Nobody ever wants to feel like a burden.

Eventually I moved out of their home, and graduated high school. I ended up graduating with my friends. Many people in the community helped me in my campaign to get back into the high school. It took convincing the principal at that time, but we did it.

When we look outside of ourselves to help others, we grow more than we can imagine because it stretches us beyond our comfort zone, it brings challenges we otherwise would never see, and in the end it forges relationships that pay dividends for a lifetime. Relationships are the pillars that hold us up when life tries to knock us down. There is no way we can navigate this obstacle course called Life alone. Since this is the case, it becomes necessary to work on our relationships. That's work, W-O-R-K. That's not go through the motions, give 85%, or pretend to be somebody you're not. *Working* on your relationships is calculated. There are a number of main characteristics that are imperative to work on if we are to have successful associations.

The first one is the hardest one for me. I am a Leo and my personality color is Red. Red Leos believe they know everything, we are always right, and the only time we are not right is when there is no debate. Well, this bit of thinking is wrong, so I guess Red Leos can be wrong. With that said, it's not easy for anybody to admit short-comings, but when we do, we set ourselves up for taking corrective action. The fact that it's not easy tells me there is a good chance it's a worthwhile endeavor.

Key Takeaways from Chapter 4

1- It is impossible to brighten somebody else's day and *not* see the light yourself. When you work to lift others up, you lift yourself up.

2- Relationships are always a two-way street. There is either progress or pain for both parties involved.

One of my favorite artists growing up was the rapper Nelly. I used to listen to his song "Heart of a Champion" during *every* gym session. In one line he says, *"If hard work pays off then easy work is worthless."* I liked how straight-forward it was. So, the journey of improving our relationships isn't easy, but there is no better way to spend your time and energy.

5
Work On You

The best project you'll ever work on is you.

From the very first episode of my podcast to today, I periodically remind listeners that it's people like them that have the greatest influence on the world around them. I say that because the people who are willing to work hard on themselves are the people that have the necessary tools to ignite passion within those around them, improve their situation, and influence just about any circumstance for the better. I am not an expert of philosophy or religion by any stretch of the imagination, but I do know enough to say that both arenas constantly challenge individuals to work on themselves. Trying to become a better version of you can never be a bad thing, ever.

Jim Rohn and Anne Frank, though they never knew each other, together they may have hit the nail on the head. Jim said, *"Work harder on yourself than you do on your job. If you work hard on your job, you can make a living. If you work hard on yourself, you can make a fortune.*" Without question, he was speaking about a fortune in terms of finances, but I don't think he meant for our minds to stop there. It's a layered idea, and if we can go beyond the surface, we'll find that fortune comes in many forms. Anne Frank said that nobody has ever become poor by giving. Seemingly counterintuitive, her words complete the idea that by giving, we are investing in future returns, literally.

Real fortunes do not come in the form of currency. Fortune is the benefit of knowing you made somebody's day better. Fortune is hearing somebody say, "Because of you, I accomplished…" Fortune is receiving a hand-written letter that thanks you for being you. If you don't take anything else from the rest of this book, please always remember this:

> Fortune is having the ability to make somebody feel fortunate that you came into their life. It's the idea that, had you never shown up, perhaps their peak happiness never would have been met. It's a sad thought, but it's only a thought, because you *are* here, and you *do* matter. At the end of the day, the betterment of oneself, is the betterment of humanity.

With this idea in mind, I want to share something very valuable I learned from being around teenagers. I have the unique opportunity to teach/coach about 150 high schoolers each day during the school year. I truly do love them. They make my days exciting, they make me laugh, and occasionally I want to scream, but we have a great time. High school students are ambitious. They have so much in their minds that they want to accomplish, and I think it's a great thing. However, in the spring of 2016, I started helping out at the local YMCA with their Teen Outreach

Program (TOP) put on by a non-profit organization called Healthy Lifestyles of Texas. On Mondays after school, we'd meet for a little over an hour. Topics for discussion ranged from goal-setting to how we should treat one another, and everything in-between.

One day during a discussion about personal goals, I kept hearing the young men talk about what shoes they wanted to get, what car they wanted to drive, what phone they were going to get next, which AAU basketball team they were going to be the next star of, and so on. There isn't anything wrong with wanting any of those things. I love nice things, and it's totally okay to have them. We kept listing goals, *none* of which were self-improvement per se.

I felt myself getting heated. For real, I was literally starting to get angry. Now, hear me out, I wasn't angry at the individuals. I was getting angry because I know what young men and women are capable of accomplishing when they put in the *effort*. And listening to them talk about "goals" that were going to be irrelevant in the near future was infuriating because they were selling themselves short.

The problem is that people, *not* just teenagers, are so worried about having a tricked out car, the latest clothes, or the newest phone. We, as a society, are literally placing our self-worth in things that don't last. If this is the case for you, then your confidence cracks when your phone cracks. Your self-image is scuffed when your basketball shoes get scuffed. Heaven forbid your brand new, $150 shoes aren't perfect. But I am telling you that if you continually invest in yourself more than you do in other things, it's impossible for you to ever be broken.

I need to make sure that you understand there is absolutely

nothing wrong with having nice things. In my opinion, nothing beats a nice new pair of comfy, cushioned Nike socks. I'm serious, there is something about a brand new pair that does it for me. I'm like a kid on Christmas when I put them on. I'm walking around with an extra pep in my step like I just got a quad shot from Starbucks. But truth be told, I'm always walking around like that, and it has nothing to do with what I am wearing. My wife can attest to the fact that I don't have bad days. I might have a bad class, a bad experience somewhere, or a bad practice, but I no longer have bad days. And I give credit to the idea of working on myself. Having a tricked out life is forever better than having a tricked out car, tricked out shoes, or a tricked out watch.

When somebody asks why they need to work on themselves, there are five simple reasons to do so. Keep in mind that these five reasons are all *in addition* to the benefit of the skills you'll acquire. These five reasons are all by-products of your effort:

1- It keeps you humble.
> It's not easy to honestly assess where you are as a person. Sometimes it's hard to admit that we have weaknesses. I can't explain how this happens, but when you do so, there is an unbridled empowerment that shows up.

2- It keeps you hungry.
> I heard one man say that we should be content with what we have, but ambitious for more. Ambition is attractive. Ambition attracts the right people, and as you know, relationships are everything.

3- Constant learning leads to constant growth, and growth leads to opportunities. No explanation needed.

4- It makes you happier.

> No man or woman has ever gone to bed and said, "I worked to improve myself today, and that was a complete waste of time." The payment for working on yourself is always two-fold. You benefit from the actual skill, but you're also paid in the confidence that comes from being disciplined enough to do difficult things.

5- You owe it to yourself, and others.

> I don't mean this in a you-deserve-it kind of way. I mean this in an it's-a-duty kind of way. This is especially true if anybody depends on you. You must try to be the best version of you that you can be, otherwise you're robbing somebody else of a better life. You don't have the right to do that. That's why you owe it to yourself and others.

Every athlete on Earth will tell you that they play harder for coaches who push their players, but also who push themselves. Regardless of the industry, or even the level for that matter, coaches, managers, CEOs, and owners get more out of their respective organizations when they are humble enough to consider their weaknesses and hungry enough to do something about them. Admitting weakness is not weakness at all. Admitting weakness is the first step in becoming a stronger person.

There is one last piece of the Work On You process that I need to mention. It's difficult, but it's rewarding. Much like working out, which releases endorphins in the brain that literally take you to a natural high, witnessing improvements in your life lights a fire that cannot be explained. Dave Ramsey, a well-known financial advisor, talks about attacking debt with "gazelle-like intensity." He shares that when you see your debt situation improving, it is energizing to work even harder to pay off debts faster.

Similarly, when you invest a little time into yourself, you start to see improvements that only make you want to work harder. Plus, if you share your goals with those around you, you have tapped into an endless source of encouragement, *if* they are the right people. That's what the next chapter is all about, making sure you are nourishing the right relationships. Nothing is worse than being cut down by those around you.

Key Takeaways from Chapter 5

1- Having an upgraded, improved life is better than having an upgraded, improved phone or car.

2- The ancient Persian poet, Rumi, said it best, *"Yesterday I was clever, so I wanted to change the world. Today I am wise, so I want to change myself."* When we improve ourselves, we improve an important piece of the world.

Just remember that the best day you can ever have is the one where you go to sleep a better person than you were when you woke up.

6
A Church Mission Call

Lessons are everywhere.

We all know how important communication is to a relationship. But, I would argue that transparency is actually the number one attribute of keeping successful connections. Communication reconciles differences, removes wedges, and helps keep a relationship strong. But transparency is the key that opens the door for communication to take place. Without it, any dialogue between people is restricted to partial truths. I learned this the hard way.

Growing up in Rigby, Idaho was a great way to experience young life. As I mentioned before, the community is close and the people are wonderful. There is a strong LDS (The Church of Jesus Christ of Latter-Day Saints aka The Mormons) population in southeast Idaho. I have always said that, though their respective citizens would disagree, southern Idaho and north Utah are basically the same place. They both have a high concentration of members of the LDS church. Actually, Rigby, Idaho is named after an early Mormon settler.

My grandparents would always take my sister and me to church on Sunday. And though I never really loved going to church, it allowed us to be very involved with our friends, their parents, and many year-round activities. We would often go on camping trips with our church group where we would learn things and do activities that at the time I thought were unnecessary, but now looking back, I realize I learned a lot in terms of problem-solving and teamwork. Our leaders were always pushing us to be better people, regularly reminding us of the high expectation we should strive for. I can't put into words how valuable those years were for me. Relationships that I will forever be grateful for were built during that time.

One relationship that started in high school was with a girl named Amanda. Our houses were separated by only the field where John would always out-ride me on his bike. The summer before our sophomore year, while sitting at John's house, I was looking through our most recent yearbook. To this day I like reading what people write in other people's yearbooks. It takes me back to the times that helped shape me into who I am today. There is a unique balance between care-freeness and caring so much when you are a teenager.

John is the cool, quiet type. He is easy to like, and that's the way he was in high school too. So, John's yearbook had its fair share of phone numbers. It wasn't unusual to swap numbers. Just a bunch of high schoolers saying, "You're nice. We should hang out. Call me." Well, thumbing through the pages, I came across Amanda's number, and asked John if I should call her. With a bit of heckling and saying that I was scared, I called her. He was right, I was scared. I was *not* the guy who was comfortable picking up the phone and calling a girl. Actually, thinking back, I am surprised to this day that I called her. But, I'm glad I did.

Amanda was a popular girl and unanimously out of my league. The thing about her, though, is she wasn't your typical popular high school girl. She was nice to everybody, and easily had one of the friendliest demeanors of her class. So, when I called her to see if she wanted to hang out, she thought nothing of it and accepted. This started a friendship that quickly turned into what would become my defining high school relationship.

As I mentioned before, Amanda is down to Earth. She comes from a family of parents and siblings who are enjoyable, funny, and strong in the LDS faith. This type of person isn't hard to be around. She and her family quickly accepted me, which was no easy task. For those who know me now, who *didn't* know 15-year-old me, you wouldn't believe my character back then. 'Character' truly is the best word to describe me in high school.

I grew close with Amanda and her family, not only because they were so accepting, but because of their support through the difficulties my mom and I were facing. They were one of those families that gave unwavering emotional encouragement that pulled me through some turbulent times. Having a seat at family dinners and being invited to family activities meant the world to me. Once again, "it takes a village" is pure truth.

I dated Amanda all throughout high school. Naturally, we discussed the future and what it might hold for our relationship. We had a plan. In the LDS church, when men turn 19 years old, they are expected to serve a two-year church mission. This is two years of proselyting somewhere in the world, away from your family and friends. Communication is limited to weekly emails and one phone call on Mother's Day and one on Christmas. I always knew that my 19th birthday was coming, but I never wanted to think about leaving for two years. I *wanted* to believe it was the right thing to do, and I could even see the value in it, I was just afraid of leaving for so long.

Amanda and I discussed it, and she clearly communicated her expectation of wanting to marry somebody who had served a mission. There is nothing wrong with that, we all have our lists of what we want in a partner. Having talked through our current and future plans, I ultimately reasoned that I should serve a mission. I wanted to.

A year after high school I moved in with my aunt Brenda and uncle Brad, both of which are very active in the church. There are certain people who are just easy to talk to. The three of us can talk for hours without even noticing it, and we have.

I remember a discussion one evening with Brenda. Having recently turned 19, she asked if I had thought about going on a mission. I told her yes, but that I had decided I wanted to focus on school at Idaho State University. She casually nodded her head in understanding, and ended the conversation with, "Well, I hope you don't close your mind off to the idea. I love you." Simple, but powerful. Fast-forward three months, late nights studying church materials, and I was submitting my paperwork to go on a mission. I had thought it through, discussed the idea with my family, friends, and of course, with Amanda. Though others gave their opinions, some for and some against, I came to my own conclusion that this was the right thing for me.

Now, it must be noted that I did *not* share the same level of belief as my family or my counterparts. For anybody familiar with LDS church meetings, you are also familiar with the phrase "I know this church is true." Well, I didn't know that, but I badly wanted to. I thought, *If I serve a mission, surely I will gain the same conviction that I hear every Sunday at church.* Having submitted my paperwork to the church, I was waiting to receive "my call," the return paperwork from the church headquarters informing me where I'd be serving for two years.

Every day I would check the mailbox. Every day I grew more anxious of where I would be going. I'd check, nothing. Check, nothing. Check, nothing. Check, nothing. It's a long, dreadful two to three weeks of waiting. Check, nothing. Check, nothing. Check, PAPERS! *"Holy sh--, I mean crap, I'll be a missionary soon, I can't say that."* I called my family and friends to notify them my papers had arrived. I was about to start my journey to belief.

(Key Takeaways from chapters 6-8 will be grouped together at the end of chapter 8)

7
Jack Johnson Made Me Do It

The heaviest burden I've ever carried was a secret.

I had friends and family gathered around to hear where I was going. I opened the papers, read aloud as my eyes went ahead to peek at the destination, *Hawaii Honolulu Mission*. "*Holy sh--, I mean crap, I am going to Hawaii!*" If I heard once, I heard it *literally* a thousand times, "*That's not a mission, that's a vacation!*" I soon started to deliver you're-not-nearly-as-clever-as-you-think-you-are looks to anybody who said that.

So the plan was to serve a two-year mission, then I would return and Amanda and I would get married soon after. Nobody trusted the plan, as "Dear John" letters are typical in this situation. Well, Amanda wasn't typical. She went to school and worked while she waited for the two years to go by. We wrote every week for two years (except for the lapse in time that I sent her a handwritten letter explaining how I had lost my wallet that contained her grandmother's ring in it. She had given it to me before I left as a reminder of our plan). Her response to the news wasn't joy by any means, but she cared less about the ring than she did my lack of communication. Emails resumed and all was well.

Her correspondence, in conjunction with my family and friends', was always uplifting and encouraging. If I was having a difficult week, I would reread old letters to get me through it. I loved Hawaii and I enjoyed the people I was with, but there was a problem: I didn't believe what I was teaching.

I wanted so badly to believe like everybody else. I would say, do, write, and pray like I thought I was supposed to. It just wasn't happening for me. I thought that maybe this was one of my struggles that I needed to work through. So I persisted.

Well, I served the best I way I knew how, fumbling my way through two years of service and growth. I like to think I came out a better person than I went in. After two years, I flew home, and hugged family and friends at the airport. I was excited for what was ahead.

I worked over the summer in Atlanta with my brother-in-law before moving to Arizona for school in the fall. While at school, Amanda was still in Idaho preparing for our wedding that was to take place in December. I made the full-day drive north to see her a few times during the semester. My struggle with belief continued and I attempted to discuss it with her, but not to the extent that I should have. I was afraid of hurting her, my family, and my friends. So, I did what I thought was best, I wasn't as transparent as I should have been.

The wedding came and we celebrated. I was genuinely happy to be marrying Amanda, but the prospect of my lack of belief having an adverse effect on our marriage limited the excitement. I thought, *I'll just keep this to myself.* Again, I didn't want to hurt anybody. What's that people say about hindsight?

We went to church and lived our lives. I continued to go to school and she worked to provide an income. Things really were going great. There was just that one detail of me not believing. It would occasionally surface through discussion, but I had never wanted to discuss it as openly as I should have. I was able to keep the problem at bay, but I was not seeing the storm I was creating by my lack of candidness. In trying to protect Amanda from the complete truth, I was causing substantially more harm to everybody, including myself.

Loneliness is defined as "sadness because one has no friends or company." Sure, that's one definition. But I was surrounded by people who I cared about and who cared deeply about me, but loneliness was my closest ally. If you've ever had to keep something from somebody you love, you know what I am talking about. If you have ever had to reconcile your inner thoughts and feelings with your external actions to keep those around you from suspecting anything, you know what I am talking about. Loneliness is not feeling like you can be you, regardless of who you are surrounded by. Loneliness has nothing to do with other people. Loneliness is simply not having yourself, because "yourself" isn't even the real you.

If you've ever cried yourself to sleep lying next to the one you love because you can't give them a genuine look in the eye, you know what I am talking about.

One weekend in the fall of 2009, we were driving from Idaho to Utah to visit my sister, Natasha, and my brother-in-law, James. It was the weekend of my nephew's birthday party. When we were only a few minutes from their house, Amanda turned to me and said, "Something is wrong with you, and I don't know what it is." She continued, "I don't know if it's me or if it's something I did, but I want to know." I knew exactly what it was, but I was too much of a coward to look her in the eye and say it. So I stayed in my head as we arrived at my sisters.

That night was relaxed. We talked and hung out with Natasha and James. I had homework from my dreadful business statistics class that I had to do, so after everybody went to bed, I started working. To this day I listen to soft music while I work. It helps me focus. This particular night I was listening to Jack Johnson. As I pushed through problems, I couldn't help but think of what Amanda said earlier. She could sense there was an issue.

She was on the couch in front of me as the light from the kitchen area spilled over to the living room where she slept. It was just enough light that I could clearly see her. I thought about how hard she worked. I thought about how caring she was. I thought about how supportive she was, not only of me, but of all her loved ones. I thought about how somebody like her didn't deserve to suffer through the unknown. As luck would have it, "Angel" by Jack Johnson came on in my headphones. I sat there and stared at somebody who had been a pillar of support for me since that first phone call at John's house years before. I stared as I watched my biggest fan sleep, likely having arrived there through heavy thoughts of *what is going on with him?* My thoughts, my feelings, my lack of transparency were as pressing as ever.

The words from Jack Johnson's song hit me:

> *I've got an angel, she doesn't wear any wings.*
> *She wears a heart that can melt my own,*
> *she wears a smile that can make me wanna sing.*
> *She gives me presents, with her presence alone.*
> *She gives me everything I could wish for,*
> *she gives kisses on the lips just for coming home.*

I continued to watch her sleep, but it all became too much. I broke down. I didn't want to tell her I had absolutely no interest in moving forward in the church, but I didn't want to keep her in limbo either. Something had to give. I knew it had to give because I was causing a lot of damage. Just a few hours earlier, she expressed that maybe *she* was the problem. She didn't know what the problem was, but she considered it was her when she asked me what was wrong. The harm of hiding your true self from those around you, *especially* your spouse, is detrimental to you, but even more so to the person in the dark. At least *I* knew what the problem was, *I* knew it wasn't her, but *she* was suffering just as much, if not more than I was. We don't have the right to keep people in the dark. Causing somebody to evaluate themselves as potentially having a problem when *I* had the problem was unjust, maybe even inhumane. Yes, it's that serious.

I tried to get myself together before I woke her. I didn't have much success. As concerned as she was before, I can't imagine what she was thinking when she woke up to me being upset.

"What's wrong?" She asked, as she sat up after seeing the state I was in. All I could do was hug her. I hugged her, told her I loved her, and cried. She hugged me back, but immediately insisted I tell her what was happening.

"I...I don't know how else to say this." I let out a

sigh that only a marriage-altering secret could create. With my head down, shoulders slumped, one hand in the other with my thumbs tapping against one another, I knew I had to get it out.

"I don't believe in the church the same way you do." I paused for a second, looked up, and said, "I actually don't believe in it all." It was out. I didn't feel the burden lift, I didn't suddenly thank myself for saying it, and I sure as hell didn't feel amazing. If anything, I felt even more terrible because I had just taken her from bad to worse.

"What about our plans?! What about our kids?! What about everything we talked about?!" Tears started for her which only made the situation more difficult for both of us. Her questions were justified and fair. All I could do was nod my head in an attempt to say, "I know, I know."

To this day it was one of the most difficult things I've had to do. Early the next morning I told Natasha, James, and my mom. We cried, we talked, we cried, we talked. It was an exhaustive sequence of events. The news was a bomb dropped on Amanda and my family. She understandably insisted that we drive home. Neither of us were really in the right state of mind to be at a birthday party.

When we arrived back in Rigby, we walked up to the front door that was opened by Amanda's mom. Without a word she gave me a hug. We didn't always see eye-to-eye on things, but that didn't stop her from supporting me, even if we didn't share beliefs.

As soon as we got inside, we sat on the couch and had a

discussion with Amanda's entire family. I remember we all shared our thoughts and feelings regarding the church. The only thing more apparent than their belief in the church was their willingness to support me in that moment.

After I told Amanda and our families, I told my closest friends, then everybody else. As soon as our families knew, a majority of my anxiety lifted, but there was still a question as to how my friends would react. These are people I've gone to church with for two decades. These are people that, had it not been for the church, I might not know. I was nervous, but if I could tell Amanda, I could tell anybody.

That's when I made a phone call to one of my best friends who changed my entire perspective in a single sentence.

8
We're Friends Because

I could've missed the pain, but I'd have had to miss the dance.
– Garth Brooks, "The Dance"

One summer, while we were working construction together, my friend Matt and I were shingling a roof. My nail gun ran out of nails for the shingles so whenever I pulled the trigger nothing but air shot out. I don't specifically remember why I did this (which is the case for a lot of the stupid things I did growing up), but I stuck the nail gun on his foot and told him I was going to nail his foot to the roof. He gave me the *you're a freaking moron* look and told me to think twice about it. Solid advice.

Well, I didn't take the advice. I pulled the trigger and as quickly as the nail gun fired, Matt jumped up in pain and grab his foot. My eyes got big and fear immediately took over as I thought that there must have been one more nail in the gun that was just waiting for me to make a terrible decision! My only hope then was that I missed the bones in his foot to decrease the healing time. Matt understandably called me a lot of names and told me how much of a fool I was. He wasn't wrong.

One minor detail of this story: Matt was only a few days away from running in the state track meet for our school. He was a sprinter, and a talented one. Well, as it turned out, there wasn't a nail in the gun. But, what *did* happen was, unbeknownst to me, a little piece of metal comes out of the end of the gun to drive the nail into the wood. So it wasn't enough to cause any real damage, but it was definitely enough to momentarily cause pain, and scare the living crap out of me, thinking I had *actually* nailed Matt's foot to the roof!

After about 10-15 seconds of jumping around and grabbing his foot, the pain eased and he casually reminded me that I wasn't the clearest thinker. We continued to work and banter in our light-hearted manner. I share that story to give you an idea of how laid-back Matt is. He has always been calm, collected, and very even-keeled. Whenever he was "mad" at me, even to this day, he usually just hits me with some verbal jabs that I *think* are insults, but he does it with a smile on his face, so sometimes it's hard to tell.

※

I went downstairs to be alone while I called Matt. I picked up the phone to dial his number. 2-0-8-#-#-#-6-2-8-8. I will never forget that cell phone number, 6-2-8-8 spells M-A-T-T. I love his narcissism.

Though he was very easy to talk to, I was still nervous about making the phone call. You never know how people are going to react. Sometimes they respond in a way that is simply impossible to predict.

Matt answered, and after the formalities of starting a conversation, I explained that there was something I needed to tell him. Like I said before, if I could get through telling Amanda, I could tell anybody. But it still wasn't easy. I tried to naturally set him up to receive the news by making small statements that I thought were necessary to ease the blow.

When I finally got to the point and told him I didn't believe in the church, I followed it up with, "I hope this doesn't change anything about our friendship."

Matt replied, "Are you *kidding* me? I'm a little offended you would say that."

Damn it, I thought. *Well, not* everybody *is going to understand.* My thoughts were cut short as his reply warranted a response from me. "Why are you offended?"

He responded in true Matt fashion with the perfect amount of wisdom and wit that I will never forget. He said, "Ali, we're not friends because we're both Mormon. We're friends because we're both really awesome and better than everybody else."

I was floored, I was relieved, and I was smiling with burden-free confusion because of what he had said. I don't tell this story to build Matt up, I tell this story for a few other reasons:

> First, nothing, and I mean *nothing* can interfere with two minds that refuse to have barriers. Matt's open-mindedness taught me that acceptance can happen even when two minds don't see eye-to-eye. He taught me that accepting others for *who* they are is substantially more important than accepting them because of *what* they believe.

51

Second, this helped me realize that I needed to trust my friends and family more. Struggles are not meant to be dealt with alone. If I had to answer the question of *What is the purpose of Family?* I would say that Family and Friends, and really all of our relationships, are there to magnify our happiness and ease the load of adversity. We're not meant to be happy alone, and surely we're not meant to struggle alone. With this said, I realize that not everybody is surrounded by a bunch of "Matts," but there are always people who rise to the occasion of supporting you.

Third, calling Matt solidified the idea of being transparent with those around me. The actual conversation I had with Matt was not nearly as bad as the burden of thinking about it. Matter of fact, that was the case for most people up to this point. Amanda, her family, and my family had been nothing short of resolutely supportive.

I said that sometimes people respond in a way that is simply impossible to predict. Well, that's true. I never could have predicted that response from Matt. There was a lot in his two sentences. He made me relax, he made laugh, but with it all, he ultimately let me know that he appreciated that I told him. He informed me that our friendship was in no way, shape, or form in jeopardy because of my belief system.

In addition to Matt, there were many other close friends and loved ones that I told, and the response was all about the same: supportive, reassuring, and optimistic. Not optimistic in the sense that everybody thought I'd start to believe the same way they do, but optimistic in terms of my relationship with them. I cannot think of a single person who didn't thank me for telling them. Matter of fact, I may have been lightly scolded once or twice for keeping the secret to myself for so long.

So I had just shared my biggest secret with those that mattered most, and It. Felt. *Incredible*! People talk about "the weight of the world," well, I know what that means. Though the discrepancy of belief was there, at least I was me.

Transparency made it possible that I could look into people's eyes without hesitation rather than fear they might somehow see into my mind and find out my secret. Transparency allows other people to say, "You don't have to go through this alone." Transparency empowers people around you in ways you will never understand until you're brave enough to be the real you. The counterfeit you can do so little, the genuine you can do so much. Regardless of who the real you is, don't apologize for it, and don't ever feel bad about it. Anybody who makes you feel like you need to suppress or minimize who you are because of *who you are* isn't somebody worthy of your time. Hear me on this: if somebody treats or speaks to you differently because of your belief system, political ideology, sexual orientation, or anything else of the sort, the problem lies with *them*, not you. Don't ever forget that.

I realize that I was fortunate in that those around me didn't expect me to change who I was. Like I said, from Amanda to my newest acquaintance, mostly everybody who mattered, supported me. Of course, in a small town people talk. And, of course, not everybody is going to agree with you, or even be tactful about how they express their disagreement. I was unable to avoid the communication of a small-town grapevine, so I heard things said by people that were hurtful. I was called fake, confused, and a coward for sharing my truth. At one point, I was told that my actions showed that I didn't really love Amanda. Do you know how hard it is to hear people who have taught you in school, church, and sports say these things about you? The thing I had to realize, though, is that the people closest to me *weren't* saying these things. The people who mattered and cared were keeping their words and actions positive. It wasn't easy, but I couldn't focus on the negativity for two reasons:

 1- People are always going to disagree. That's part of life. There are over 7 Billion people on Earth, so you're bound to have one or two that won't get where you're coming from. We have to learn how to say, "I understand, we disagree. And that is totally okay."

 2- If the relationship isn't important, then the opinion from that person isn't important. Too often we place so much value in things, opinions, and people who really aren't relevant to *our* lives. Wasting time and energy on the opinion of others when those people add nothing to our life is literally throwing life away.

When I heard what somebody said or what somebody thought and it wasn't pretty, I tried to smile, nod my head, and move on. If we want the luxury of having our own opinions, we better be willing to afford those around us the same luxury. I must emphasize, it's not easy, but it's necessary. To this day I can let myself get worked up about some of the things that were said, but in the end, those things can't matter.

So everything was great then, right? Wrong. Telling everybody about my secret lifted a weight off of my shoulders, but that weight was subsequently dropped into life's ocean that caused massive waves. The marriage between me and Amanda felt those waves, and after a decade of being together, nearly five of which were marriage, we went our separate ways.

To this day, it might be the most difficult thing I have ever had to go through. A divorce at the age of 26 from somebody who had been nothing but a constant support in my life seemed unfathomable. But, it had to be.

We wrote each other a letter, sharing final thoughts. In mine, I saw it fit to share with her what Jim Rohn wrote to his former wife, in his final letter to her:

> *"I wish for you and I wish the best for you, and I understand that dilemma."*

I could not sever my ties with the church but keep my ties with Amanda. One thing I respect about the LDS church is that, for them it's not a Sunday thing, it's a lifetime thing. I do not regret being transparent. It is the best way to live. I do not regret believing the way I do. My belief is the result of my own study and my own reasoning, therefore, it just is. Any relationship that makes you stronger is a relationship you should cherish.

I don't regret picking up the phone that summer day in 2000 at John's house and dialing Amanda's number. It provided me with a relationship that opened my eyes to what great support feels like.

Key Takeaways from Chapters 6-8

1- Our strongest support systems might come from the people we least expect. Being transparent allows others to support you.

2- Suppressing issues will never make them go away. Matter of fact, suppressing problems is the prime environment for them to grow bigger and more difficult to deal with.

3- If we don't take care of our problems, insecurities, and questions, it may make others feel like *they* have a problem. That is simply not fair.

4- Working through difficulties identifies those who love and appreciate you as a person.

9
Beth

Trust is established through dialogue.
— Paulo Friere

Being transparent with family is a must. They're family, they deserve it. When it comes to everybody else, I won't say that we have to be an open book, but transparency is still key.

As a teacher, being open and honest with my students builds more bridges and strengthens my relationship with them in ways that transcend the latest and greatest new technique to try out, often called "best practices." For example, if I am having a rough couple of hours, and I anticipate a high-energy class, I will explicitly state where I am at in terms of my mood. On several occasions, I have stood at the front of my classroom and said, "Heads up, please. On a typical day, my fuse is this long (using my hands as a measure of an imaginary two-foot fuse in front of me). Today, my fuse is much shorter. I'm probably somewhere around here (cutting the fuse to just inches). I am simply telling you this to give you an idea of where I'm at." It amazes me what this simple communication does for the class. It gives them some insight into my mood, instead of them wondering why the heck I am being a grump that day.

This is a simple practice I use to communicate with my students. Again, it's transparency. In this situation transparency is not necessarily make or break, but in some situations it can be.

Every school has students that push the limits. I am not talking about the class clowns, the bullies, or the wannabe tough guys. I am talking about the at-risk students who don't get to eat, have parents in and out of jail, use drugs, and view teachers in the same way they view any other authority figure: not considering their best interests and out to get them.

I am fortunate to work at a school that has its fair share of this population. I researched all area schools and settled on Theodore Roosevelt High School because of its specific demographic. I have the best "job" in the world.

During my second year of teaching I was introduced to a student who we will call Beth. Beth came from a house that no young lady should have to grow up in. Instability was the only constant in Beth's life. She made "friends" in my class, but not the kind of friends that hung out on the weekends. Beth didn't keep anything a secret. Outwardly, Beth seemed transparent, but I came to learn that she had some heavy burdens. If she didn't like you, she didn't hesitate to say so. If she didn't want to be in class, she'd stand up, say, "[Forget] this [crap]," and walk out, tearing posters off my wall as she did so. If she didn't like another student, her resolution was to fight in the courtyard at lunch. At the end of the day, reasoning with Beth was seemingly impossible.

I continued to work with her, letting her know that I was there for her when she wanted help on her math, or if she just wanted to talk. As teachers, we are lectured about how we are *teachers*. We're told, "You're not a counselor, you're not an administrator, you're their teacher." Yeah, right. Whatever.

Being a classroom teacher who effectively connects with students means putting on 12 different hats throughout the day. With Beth, sometimes I was an Algebra teacher, sometimes I was her basketball conversationalist, sometimes I was her ear that listened to how badly she hates cops, and sometimes I was the opposition in a Tupac-is-better-than-Biggie debate (I like to think I won that debate. Which side of that argument I am on is irrelevant to this book, so I won't share, but I will say that you have to Keep Ya Head Up because Life Goes On and at the end of the day Only God Can Judge Me).

In the limited number of times Beth came to class, she and I built a good relationship. It wasn't a no-walls-are-up relationship, but I got to the point where she would at least *consider* what I was saying.

One day, I ran into one of my coworkers who was shaking his head and immediately asked, "Can you believe this? When did we lose control of the school?"

"What do you mean?" I asked.

"Beth just came through this hallway pissed off, ripped down every poster, and said nobody was going to do shit about it!"

I looked around and saw the aftermath of Beth.

"Where'd she go?"

"She's right there," my coworker pointed.

I looked outside to the left and spotted her walking alongside the cafeteria. To the right, across the courtyard, stood a couple of administrators and our school police officers. I debated whether or not I should go outside and try to talk to Beth. She was out of class, obviously upset about something, and presumably in no mood to talk to a teacher. But, I went anyway.

As I approached her, before I could get a word out, a long list of expletives and invitations to leave her alone flew my way. I expected it. I waited for the storm of words to pass, then when she stopped, I softly asked, "What's going on, Beth? Why are you mad?"

15 minutes later, the two of us were sitting across from one another on some cafeteria tables outside. She was in tears telling me about how our administration and police officers betrayed her. Without going into detail, they were legally bound to share certain information with the proper authorities that Beth had told them earlier. All I could do was listen and try to calm her down. I didn't feel like I was anywhere near succeeding.

After a while, one of the assistant principals came up to me and asked if I would escort Beth to the office where her father was waiting. I told him yes, not knowing if it was going to happen. With more tears and resistance, we yo-yo'd our way to the office. Taking 10 steps forward and five steps back at every time she thought of going home. Nobody ever makes Beth do anything, so I am glad she decided to go.

We finally made it inside the building where Beth and I sat outside a counselor's office and listened to her father complain, degrade, and belittle his daughter. I was stunned. I really couldn't believe what I was hearing her dad say.

"All she causes is trouble. She's loud, she starts fights, she's a troublemaker! The girl knows better! She's just selfish. Don't care about anybody but herself!" I shot a look at Beth, hoping that somehow she couldn't hear. I knew better, though. She had her head in her hands, rocking back and forth, crying. No father should ever speak about his child like that.

Suddenly, I could hardly blame Beth for anything. If you would've heard everything he was saying, you'd agree. I don't excuse her actions, but I understand them. Parents, authority figures, and people in the position of influence must be aware of the effect their words have on those they reach.

It made so much sense. The reason for all the acting out, all the mood swings, all the struggle in the classroom came into focus. To this day, I have only shared the story about my mom with one student. It was Beth. As we were sitting there, I felt betrayed for her. I never had to deal with something like this. As tough as times had been, I at least had two parents who loved me and showed it. Beth didn't have that.

I opened up to Beth about how I felt when my mom attempted suicide. Some of my emotion from the past surfaced as I told her the story and how it made me feel. I could see in Beth's eyes the realization that perhaps I was a human with feelings as well, and not just some programmed robot teacher that many students think we are. Her crying stopped as she listened. The transparency was evident, the walls no longer existed. After I finished, she explained to me *why* she didn't want to go home: abuse, in all forms, and drugs were the norm.

Beth left with her father that day who I later found out was "her rock." It's fascinating to me how tightly we can hold onto unhealthy relationships, but, I guess a parent-child bond is something different.

A few months later I saw Beth on campus. She was back for what would be a quick stay as a student before she was sent back to alternative high school again. I gave her an energetic, "What's up, Beth?!" And she responded with, "What's going on, Mr. G?" I was in a rush to after-school practice, so I gave her a high-five in passing. As I was walking away I heard her say to her friends, "That has to be, like, the only cool teacher out here."

I don't share that to boast. Beth said whatever she wanted, whenever she wanted, regardless of circumstance, and it usually was dependent on her mood. But I share that to emphasize how important and effective transparency is. If we are to have healthy, beneficial relationships, we have to be steadfast in keeping open and honest dialogue with those who matter. If an Iranian-American country boy from small-town Idaho can build a relationship with an at-risk teenager from a low-income, public school in a city of 1.3 million people, then you can build any relationship you want.

If any of your relationships aren't as strong as you'd like them to be, I'd ask you to consider how transparent are you being? You can't have a 100% relationship when you're being 80% you.

I share some of these moments with you in order to showcase the benefit of being transparent. I find it ironic that the best way to talk about transparency, is by being transparent.

Up to this point, I have shared some very personal moments that have hopefully shed light on some necessary ideas, i.e., the importance of our relationships, the benefit of healthy relationships, and why it's imperative to be transparent. I can't go on without discussing a quality I greatly admire in others. This could very well be one thing that has the potential to ruin any chance of a successful relationship before it even starts, and it starts with you.

Key Takeaways from Chapter 9

1- Everybody, and I mean *everybody* can be reached. Through dialogue and patience, any two people can build a relationship that is mutually beneficial.

2- Although being vulnerable feels uncomfortable, there is power in openness and transparency. We have all heard that nobody cares how much you know until they know how much you care. Once somebody realizes that you care about them, genuinely, they allow you to speak to them differently.

10
Sylvester Stallone Got Me Paid

If you don't ask, you don't get.
— Stevie Wonder

"So you're asking for a raise before you even get the job, did I hear that correctly?"

"I mean, that's one way to look at it."

"And what's the other way?" This wasn't going quite as I had planned.

"I completely understand why you typically start new tellers at $8 per hour. The training, the mistakes, the slower transaction times, the inability to thoroughly answer client questions, and so on. I *completely* get that. Not only do I get it, I agree with it!"

"And you're a new teller…er, possibly a new teller, and you just said you agree with paying new tellers $8 per hour. So why exactly are you asking for a raise?"

"Well, technically I'm not asking for a raise--"

"Yeah, yeah…You know what I mean."

"Alright, I said I understand why you *typically* start new tellers at that rate, but--"

"But you're not a typical new teller?" Being cut off twice in a row was a bit frustrating, but I had to answer her question.

"Correct."

"Okay, I am all ears, what is *atypical* about you in regards to being a teller?"

When the HR rep asked this question, I knew I had it in the bag. I had applied for a bank teller job while I was in college. I received a phone call for a first interview that went really well. I was told I'd be receiving a second phone call from HR to discuss the possibility of when I'd be starting, the compensation plan, and the rest of the hiring details. The bank wanted to start me at the same rate they started everybody else. Here's the problem: I'm not everybody else, at least I didn't think so. So, I did what I thought everybody in a phone interview should do, I quoted Sylvester Stallone in the movie series *Rocky*.

"Have you ever seen any of the *Rocky* movies?" I asked.

"Ummm, I don't know, probably, but I don't remember."

"Well, there is a part in one of the movies where Sylvester Stallone is lecturing his son about life. He tells his son, 'If you know what you're worth, go out and get what you're worth.' Basically he is telling his son that if he doesn't like or agree with something, to do something about it. I like the idea of starting *typical* new tellers at $8 per hour. I do. The bank is doing that exactly right."

"I feel a 'but' coming."

"*But* I have worked in retail, in restaurants, and have cold-called people on their doorsteps for almost a decade in combined experience. During that time I learned how to talk to people. I learned how to read people. I learned how to make people feel comfortable while they were giving me there social security number and credit card information on their doorstep."

"Yeah, I'd never do that."

"Well, I've never knocked on your door, but that's beside the point." I said it jokingly enough that the lightness of the comment outweighed its arrogance. "Whether I am discussing the most effective cleaning solution with a custodian or which account yields the highest return given a certain risk tolerance of a Fortune 500 CEO, I can make people feel comfortable. And that's what banking is, making people feel comfortable that their hard-earned money is in our hands. Will it take me a week or so to learn the system? Absolutely. But based on my current skillset, once I do learn the system, I will be readily equipped to serve even your most diverse member."

I nailed it. I knew the phone call was coming. I knew what the phone call was going to be about. I knew what they were looking for. I knew what their vision was. I knew it was my only opportunity to "go out and get what I was worth" (with that said, no hourly rate will ever define any of us – we are worth *way* more). The bank started me out at $2 more per hour than a typical new hire. I'm not a math genius but I know enough to recognize that was a 25% raise before my first day!

So why do I tell you this? What relevance does it have in terms of relationships? Well, my relationship with the bank started good and ended great. Initially, the conversation with HR was a bit rockier than I had anticipated (See what I did there? Seriously, I murder puns). But eventually I was able to communicate why I felt like I deserved the higher pay. HR saw the value in that, and we moved forward with it.

The *only* reason asking for a "raise" worked out is because I really did bring an ability to build relationships, make customers feel comfortable, and I brought the ability to clearly communicate. I added value to their branches by being somebody who was willing and able to talk to all people, and most importantly, make them feel comfortable with the bank. Had I asked for the "raise" without having a justifiable reason to do so, they would have hung up the phone mid-interview. Did I embellish my approach a little bit by using some of their terminology when I don't really speak like that? Sure. But I knew that banks care about returns, risk tolerance, and relationships above all else. And I felt like I actually could bring value to their branches.

Most problems I have seen in a relationships, whether it be school, work, sports, or somebody's personal life, arose from one or more people advertising themselves as more than they were. We can't ask for a top-tier compensation plan but then show up with a mediocre skillset and a sub-par work ethic.

So why then do some people treat their relationships this way? These leeches of life take, take, and take, but when you ask them for a dime it's like you asked for the world. We will get more into this later.

Notice that Sylvester Stallone didn't tell his son to go out and get *more* than he was worth. That's called being a fake, a phony, and a fraud. You have every right to ask for what is rightfully yours, but only *after* you earn it. So you want strong, healthy connections with quality people? Become a quality person who is worthy of strong, healthy connections. The equation is simple, the implementation is a bit more taxing.

In my story about the bank, imagine you are me, and the bank is a relationship you care about. I knew I wanted to work for the bank. I also knew how much the bank planned on paying me to start out. Most importantly, I knew what mattered to the bank. Banks, like every other entity in the service industry, are focused on relationships. Somebody might say, "No, they're focused on money!" Sure, but relationships drive the bottom line. Relationships = Business = Money.

I knew if I could convince HR that I could strengthen their client relationships while being an efficient, reliable employee, they'd see the value in paying me more. It was a win-win relationship.

That's exactly what we need to do with those around us. We must know what people care about. What drives them? Why do they get up in the morning? What influences them? What are their concerns? Once we know these things, we must ensure we are the type of person who is able to fulfill the need.

Really, at the end of the day, we keep people in our lives because they fulfill a certain need for us. It sounds selfish, but we are selfish creatures. But, the healthiest relationships are the ones that are *mutually*-beneficial.

Key Takeaways from Chapter 10

1- We cannot expect more *out* of a relationship than we are willing to put *in*.

2- For a relationship to work, *both* parties involved must receive some benefit. I wouldn't have worked for the bank if I didn't feel like the compensation was relatively fair, and they wouldn't have hired me if they didn't feel the same. The greater the give-to-receive ratio, the greater chance of success.

I wasn't boastful with my words when speaking to HR, but I wasn't being modest. I was simply speaking what I felt. That leads me to arguably the most influential attribute in society. If you have this one thing, you can do anything you want to.

11
A Fraud and a Check

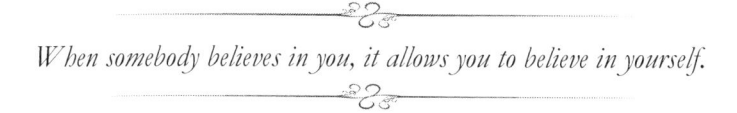

When somebody believes in you, it allows you to believe in yourself.

A while back I came across a story that teaches a vitally important attribute to success in any endeavor. It goes as follows:

> A business executive was deep in debt and could see no way out. Creditors were closing in on him. Suppliers were demanding payment. He sat on the park bench, head in hands, wondering if anything could save his company from bankruptcy. Suddenly an old man appeared before him.
>
> "I can see that something is troubling you," he said. After listening to the executive's woes, the old man said, "I believe I can help you." He asked the man his name, wrote out a check, and pushed it into his hand saying, "Take this money. Meet me here exactly one year from today, and you can pay me back at that time." Then he

turned and disappeared as quickly as he had come.

The business executive saw in his hand a check for $500,000, signed by John D. Rockefeller, one of the richest men in the world at that time! "I can erase my money worries in an instant!" He realized. But instead, the executive decided to put the uncashed check in his safe. Simply knowing it was there might give him the strength to work out a way to save his business, he thought.

With renewed optimism, he negotiated better deals and extended terms of payment. He closed several big sales. Within a few months, he was out of debt and making money once again. Exactly one year later, he returned to the park with the uncashed check. At the agreed-upon time, the old man appeared. But just as the executive was about to hand back the check and share his success story, a nurse came running up and grabbed the old man.

"I'm so glad I caught him!" she cried. "I hope he hasn't been bothering you. He's always escaping from the rest home and telling people he's John D. Rockefeller." And she led the old man away by the arm.

The astonished executive just stood there, stunned. All year long he'd been wheeling and dealing, buying and selling, convinced he had half a million dollars behind him. Suddenly, he realized that it wasn't the money, real or imagined, that had turned his life around. It was his newfound self-confidence that gave him the power to achieve anything he went after.

I like this story because it actually teaches several lessons, but the obvious one is that confidence is key. The day that the struggling business executive was handed a check for a half-million dollars, he hadn't done anything to improve his skillset, he hadn't changed his list of prospects, and he wasn't offering something different in terms of his product. What he did have, though, was a belief in himself. And that belief in himself literally changed everything for him. It changed his mentality which changed his approach with those he did business with, and that changed his financial situation. It wasn't anything tangible. It was all in his head. All he needed was a little boost in confidence.

I see lack of belief in people every day. Whether they are young or old, I see people walking through life with their head down. Maybe not literally, but I can see it in their eyes, I can hear it in their words. I have students, fellow teachers, and people in my personal life who I want to shake to snap them out of their own disbelief! You were born with the same brain and heart as some of the world's greatest leaders. I don't know a lot, but I do know we all have something very special to offer those around us if we're willing to do so.

At the end of 2015, I went to a conference put on by world-renowned speaker, Dr. Eric Thomas. His right-hand man, CJ, was there as well. The two of them held a private meeting before the main session for a small group of people.

After the first session, I went up to talk to CJ. Like talking to one of my buddies, the conversation was natural and easy. I share this because I have met people who are household names who act completely different in person.

This isn't the case for anybody in their organization. As we chatted, I asked him my favorite question: 20 seconds, what's your best advice? I handed him the book I was holding, *Greatness Is Upon You* by Dr. Eric Thomas. He thought for maybe two or three seconds then said, "Yeah, I got you."

This is what he wrote:

Handwritten note: "What you have is plenty."

Five simple words.

- These five words should be told to every student who doesn't believe they're smart enough.

- These five words should be told to every athlete who doesn't believe they're skilled enough.

- These five words should be told to every employee who doesn't know if they're capable.

- These five words should be told to every young man who measures himself against others.

> -And these five words should be told to every young woman who thinks her self-worth is based on a skewed societal standard that is ignorant of what beauty really is.

When CJ wrote that, I thanked him, and we had to make our way to the other conference room for the next session. As I sat waiting for it to start, I thought about what those words meant. **What you have is plenty**. There is so much depth in that thought.

I had been toying with the idea of creating a website where I could share my blog and podcasts, but hadn't because I would always talk myself out of it. I would justify that I should wait until this, that, or the other. Really, though, I wasn't sure of myself. Frankly put, I wasn't confident I could create and sustain it.

The more those words sat with me, the more I furrowed my brow and asked, "Why *not* me? Why can't I share my ideas with people in hopes to somehow help them? What if somebody *did* benefit from it?" I feel like his words gave me the little shot of confidence that I needed to push me to *act* on the decision. He seemed so confident in writing it that it's as if his confidence rubbed off on me. We've all heard before that confidence is contagious, and that was a prime example of how.

<hr>

We have all seen a guy holding the hand of the pretty girl next to him and have all thought the same thing, *Why is she with* him?! You know it, and I know it, and don't ever try to deny it. The girl is beautiful, and the guy is not, at all. It sounds harsh, but it's true: Not-so-pretty guys with very pretty girls is common. We sit and scratch our heads questioning the situation, but the answer is obvious. In every single one of these scenarios, the guy will have one thing, confidence.

I need to be clear on something here. I am not suggesting we walk around with our noses up acting like we're God's gift to Earth, but there is something to be said about a person who stands tall, with their shoulders back, and makes eye contact. Confidence, not arrogance.

One of my favorite displays of confidence comes from two men from the United Kingdom who travelled to Las Vegas for the highly-promoted Floyd Mayweather/Manny Pacquiao fight in 2015. Chris Stowe and Ifran Ahmad purchased $1,000 tickets that would admit them to nose-bleed seats at the MGM Grand to watch the fight. However, in addition to arriving with their tickets, they showed up in track suits and hats that looked exactly like Floyd Mayweather's entire team.

When Mayweather and company were on their way into the fight, the two risk-takers latched on the back of the posse and walked in like they were childhood friends of Floyd Mayweather. They had purchased tickets, so watching the fight is watching the fight, right? Wrong. Instead of watching the fight through binoculars from the top of the arena, they watched the fight from ringside seats that were selling for over $800,000 per seat!

The story didn't stop when the fight ended. No, the two friends proceeded to stay with the group and the A-list peppered after-party.

Now, I am not advocating being deceptive. I am simply pointing out that when carry yourself with confidence, people look at you differently. And, sometimes, your perspective changes as well, literally.

⁂

The story of the business executive and the two men who attended a highly promoted fight are two examples of what confidence can do for you. And again, I am not promoting being deceptive and sneaking your way into any event, I am simply shedding light on how confidence *can be* a game-changer. I emphasize *can be* because confidence isn't a cure-all.

Confidence doesn't kill doubt. Confidence doesn't eliminate fear. Confidence can and does coexist with anxiety. It is critical to understand that when you feel these negative emotions, to not start doubting yourself. It's during these crucial times that we need to engage the confidence we have to see us through the moment. Remember: head up, shoulders back, and face the situation.

When our confidence (read: belief) is bigger than our doubts, we act. The more we act, the more confidence we gain. The closer our lives are lined up with our core values, the more assurance we have. The more our outer-self mimics who our inner-self is, the more we walk with certainty.

When it's all said and done, we are the most confident when we are who we say we are. Of all the relationships we have, our relationship with ourselves is the most important one. When this relationship is out of balance, none of our other relationships can be in balance. Confidence in oneself is the primer for any meaningful progress.

Key Takeaways from Chapter 11

1- Confidence can be the one factor in turning a bad situation into a great one.

2- You are justified in walking with confidence. Remember, "What you have is plenty." I say it in my podcast and I will continue to spread the idea that *nobody has had the same experience you have had, therefore* nobody *can influence others the way* you *do.*

3- Confidence can take you places you otherwise would never have the opportunity to go.

4- Confidence does not automatically get rid of self-doubt, fear, etc. Confidence gives you the zeal to move forward through adversity and to not stop because of the unknown. Doubt and fear will always be a part of life, but they don't have to stop us from accomplishing our goals.

5- When you are the most genuine version of you, you set yourself up to cultivate self-confidence.

12
Respect Your Elders Is Dead

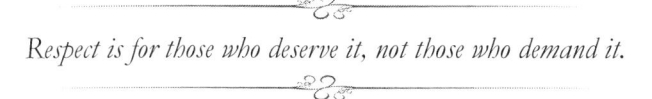

Respect is for those who deserve it, not those who demand it.

I am excited to get into my favorite part of this book, but first we need to cover something that all people must understand. Whether you're the leader of a business, a team, a classroom, a family, or a university, we must all understand respect. And I am talking about *mutual, two-way* respect. Again, some of you are probably thinking, *Duh, Ali, everybody understands this*. But the fact of the matter is that everybody *doesn't* understand this.

I heard a knock on my classroom door, but before I could make my way over to open it, a fellow teacher stuck her head in and, with teary eyes, asked if I had a second. My co-teacher and I looked at each other, she gave me an I've-got-you-covered nod, and I stepped outside.

The Golden Connection

Standing in the hallway, my colleague proceeded to explain to me why she was so upset. She had been working hard with one particular student, we'll call him Tyler, who seemed to not appreciate any of her help. She went on to explain that she *worked*, and *pleaded*, and *begged*, and *worked*, and *pleaded*, and *begged*, and *worked*, and *pleaded*…you get the idea. And not only did she feel like Tyler wasn't responding, she felt completely disrespected and, in her words, "shit on." She asked me why he was acting this way, and if he ever treated me the same. We shared him as a student, and I must say that interaction with Tyler wasn't always easy. Sometimes it did feel like he didn't appreciate the help he was given, but he was a teenage boy who came from a home that would be difficult for anybody to thrive in.

I assured her that her efforts weren't in vain. I told her that we don't always see the return on our investments in students, but that we have to keep investing anyway. She calmed down, said thank you, and we both went back to our respective classrooms.

Fast-forward a few days, I was walking back to class from my conference period. I turned the corner to head to my room and right in front of me I saw exactly "why Tyler was acting [that] way." With a finger in his face and a tone that said "You *will* listen," this same teacher, who just days ago was baffled as to why his response wasn't favorable, had Tyler's back against the lockers and was chewing him up one side and down the other while stating, "You *do not* talk to me like that! I'm a teacher!" Now, I wasn't in the classroom to see what sparked this reaction from her, but I have seen enough in the classroom, in the workplace, and in my personal life to know that there is a way to talk to somebody, and a way *not* to talk to somebody. Regardless of position, we are all human beings and we respond favorably to feeling respected.

For any relationship to work, there must be mutual respect. The most influential leaders are the ones who respect those within their domain. That's not to say authority cannot be exercised. There is a time and a place for calculated power. Matter of fact, it is necessary. But the sooner we understand a few things, the easier life and relationships get.

First, nobody respects anybody because of their position. Whether Republican or Democrat, even the President of the United States, arguably the most powerful position on Earth, is the target of heavy criticisms. So for a teacher to think they're immune to disrespect because "they are a teacher," is naïve at best.

Second, the world doesn't respect people because of their age. This may have been be the case a few decades ago. I know that it definitely was when I was growing up.

One day I walked into the living room at my grandparent's house where my grandpa was watching TV. I asked him if we could watch something else. I'll never forget what he said to me. He instructed, "Kids don't choose what adults get to watch." That was the end of the discussion. When a grandparent spoke, that was that. As a former boxer in the Marines, my grandpa wasn't worried about tact, he was direct. That was in the early 90's. Today, two decades later, we find ourselves in a different world.

As I said before, we respect those who respect us. I have had many conversations about the fact that the last generation to adopt "respect your elders" has been born. The future of earning respect from those around us will be primarily based on how we treat them. Whether this is a good thing or a bad thing, it's a thing. And if you don't believe me, spend one day with anybody born after 1990.

Finally, one more important fact to understand is that nobody really cares about your accomplishments, let alone is willing to respect you because of them. So regardless of your position, age, or your accomplishments, focusing on *giving* respect is a prerequisite to *receiving* respect.

Respect can be a tricky course to work through. There has to be a balance. We can respect opinions without agreeing with them, we can respect actions without condoning them, and we can respect an idea without endorsing it. Though it's tricky, it's possible to do.

Being on a high school campus, it is inevitable that you will come across some fights. Sometimes they're just verbal disagreements, and sometimes you're trying to calculate exactly when to jump in to break up a physical altercation while not trying to catch a fist to your own face. During my time in education, I have found that deescalating a situation is *all* about respect and understanding.

Anytime two people disagree, it's because there is a discrepancy in their viewpoints. Whether it's a couple, coworkers, or some athletes, disagreements arise. How those disagreements are handled dictates whether the relationships will move forward in success or be restricted by an inability to respect another's opinion. Here is what I have found: We *must* learn how to say "I understand." The best setting to nurture a feeling of mutual respect is an environment of understanding.

One day, a fight broke out in the hallway between two students. I didn't know either of them. Naturally, I dropped my items, got between the two of them and before I knew it, another teacher had stepped in to help. He had one kid, I had the other.

In these heated moments, you can look into their eyes and see that logic and reason are completely absent. In these moments, telling a teenager to "make good decisions" so that they can "avoid suspension" is about as effective as glasses for the blind. All the kid wanted to do was bloody the face of his opponent.

With the two of us staying between them, I did my best to get the attention of the student I was holding back. I told him I understood why he wanted to fight. I did my best to tell him, "I get it." I said. "You're pissed off! That makes sense. I understand that you're mad." He responded, "No! He won't stop running his mouth…" At this point, we had separated the two enough that it was over. "He's talking shit and then gets mad when I do something!"

"I get it! I'd want to punch him in the face too!" With that, it was as if I had just slapped him. He looked at me, almost confused, so I jumped on it. "I totally understand why you're mad. People run their mouth, it's annoying, and you want to rearrange their face. *Trust me*, I know exactly where you're coming from! Like, it makes sense!" I knew that if I could get him to understand that I *understood* why he was feeling that certain way, I could get him to listen to me. But if he felt like I didn't understand his frustration, his "logic," then I'd have no power to influence any of his thoughts.

We settled down, and I gave him a chance to explain himself and his side of the story. Within minutes he was calm. I still didn't know his name, but here we were discussing options for how to better handle problematic situations in the future. I believe the *only* way we got to that point is because there was a level of understanding. I made it clear that I didn't *agree* with his actions, but I *understood* them, and that made all the difference.

The example of a physical altercation may seem a bit extreme, but if principles will work in extreme situations, then simple verbal disagreements will be a breeze to handle when tensions may not be as high. Making somebody feel understood is the first step to making them feel respected. Once they feel respected, people afford you the opportunity to give them your input. If you passionately respect those around you, you can passionately instruct and correct them. If you lack this respect, though, you will have no ability to have such an influence.

To clarify, saying "I understand" is not the same as saying "I agree." It's important for us to recognize why our kids throw a fit, why our spouses are upset, why our bosses are mad, and why our colleagues make some of the decisions they do. We don't have to agree with them, but understanding them will help build a mutual respect that can't help but benefit the relationship.

Key Takeaways from Chapter 12

1- Nobody is going to respect you because of your age, title, or accomplishments.

2- When people know that we respect them, we have the power to influence them for the better.

3- Learning how to say "I understand" will expedite the process of creating an environment of mutual respect.

13
Dialogue Is Everything

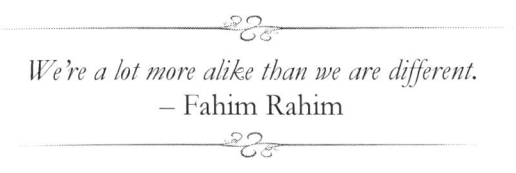

We're a lot more alike than we are different.
– Fahim Rahim

In June 2016, I flew to Columbus to do some work. I had some free time; so, I decided to explore. I drove around, not knowing where I was going. I just wanted to sight-see and check out Columbus, unrestricted.

After about 15-20 minutes of aimless driving, I found myself in a pretty run-down looking area. People were on their front steps hanging out, listening to music, and seemingly just passing the day. I drove past two people sitting on a small rock wall with their stroller. I continued to observe the area, all the while I couldn't help but notice that I was being observed. I mean, I am not surprised. As I checked out my surroundings I was driving slower than usual, and that probably looked a bit odd.

I had made my way to a part of Columbus that you won't see on a travel brochure. Bent chain-link fences, bars on convenient store doors and windows, vacant buildings, sporadic tagging, unkempt yards, etc. were the most typical scenery. I parked the car, grabbed my black leather 5"x 8" book that I used to take notes, and started to walk the sidewalk. Earlier in the day I had been walking around Ohio State's campus asking random people what advice they'd give me if they only had 20 seconds to do so. I had the same objective in this neighborhood.

This was a predominantly black neighborhood, and it was very obvious to me that it's not typical for somebody to walk those sidewalks asking random people their best advice. That's what made it fun: asking people I didn't know an off-the-wall question for seemingly no reason.

I walked, gave a respectful downward head nod when somebody looked my way, and continued on my way. I was walking toward a couple and their baby when the guy jokingly said, "You've got to be the only white boy out here!" His wife slapped his arm and told him to stop it. I laughed and returned, "Then that must make me the coolest white boy out here!" They both appreciated the humor in it. I stopped and met Tony, Angel, and their little boy. I forgot their boy's name, but he was in a stroller that was faced away from me at an angle. He kept sticking out half of his face in a peek-a-boo manner, only to hide again once he saw me looking.

Tony saw my little book and asked what I was doing. I told him why I was in Columbus and proceeded to ask him my question. They both thought for a second. With a crooked smile on her face, and a tilted head, Angel said, "I don't...really know, honestly."

"You only have 15 more seconds, and I need some advice," I reminded. "What do you tell me?"

"Okay, be safe...be blessed...Nobody is promised

Dialogue Is Everything

tomorrow." Angel answered.

"Be safe, be blessed," I repeated. "I love it." Tony immediately added on, "Yeah, and live life. Be you. Tell 'em who you are!" Be safe. Be blessed. Live life. Be you. Advice can't get much better than that.

Tony and Angel were a highlight in my trip to Columbus. Two hardworking parents who were struggling to make ends meet, but they still had wonderful perspective.

Before I left, Tony asked why I was in their neighborhood specifically. I told him I had just hopped in my car and started driving. He laughed and asked, "Then you just parked and decided it was a good idea to start walking up and down *these* streets?" I could tell he was a bit perplexed. I smiled and said yes. He added, "Maybe you are the coolest white boy out here!" We all laughed. I am not suggesting you drive to the roughest area in your city and approach complete strangers. But I do agree with Dr. Fahim Rahim when he says "there is more good in the world than bad."

I gave Tony and Angel each a hug, and tried to give their son a fist bump, but he was still in full peek-a-boo mode. The fist bump will have to wait.

I share this story because, before I stopped to get to know Tony and Angel, they were two people and a stroller. What we must do better as members of society is to *learn* about others. Learn to identify with them. When we can identify with others, even others who seem different than us, our lives are enriched by the addition of another relationship, another way of thinking, and another connection to the rest of humanity. I will likely never see Tony and Angel again in my life. But they added to it. They made my life better. One day I will have kids of my own, and

The Golden Connection

I will tell them this story. I hope to instill in them the idea that everybody has something to offer.

Key Takeaways from Tony & Angel

1- When you talk to somebody, you learn.

2- When you learn, the possibility for misunderstanding is diminished.

3- Everybody has a story. Everybody has goals, dreams, and ambitions. *Everybody* is *somebody*.

4- Only when a child is ready will he give you a fist bump.

Be safe. Be blessed. Live life. Be you.

14
Theory of Resources

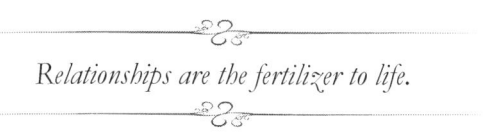

Relationships are the fertilizer to life.

During the summer of 2013, I had the opportunity to work as a mentor to a young man named Caden, who is now a very close friend of mine. During our time together, I shared an idea with him that sort of regulates the relationships I keep. It's called the Theory of Resources, and it helped me realize that we simply don't have time for everybody. It may sound harsh, but the truth can be harsh.

Our lives are rich with resources. For pretty much any problem we face, there is a resource to help us through it. For any question we have, there is a resource to help us find an answer. I thought about this, and concluded that our four most critical resources are time, energy, knowledge, and money.

Our interaction with these four resources is two-way, we are enabled by them, but they also restrict us to a degree.

How these resources enable us

- Time is the most valuable resource. It gives us the chance to pursue, to do, and to achieve.
- Energy is what enables us to do our work.
- Knowledge is having the information. This allows us to solve, create, and improve situations.
- Money gives us access to other tools to use. Sometimes it gives us access to more knowledge, and sometimes it frees up our time by allowing us to outsource some of our work.

How these resources restrict us

- Time: when we are out, we are out. Unrenewable, we *must* learn to utilize this effectively.
- Energy, knowledge, and money are all restrictors when we don't have a sufficient amount of any of them. For example, you might have all the energy to build a house and have all the money to do so, but if you don't have the knowledge, not a single wall can be built.

Theory of Resources

You are in the middle of this box of resources. Think of your life like this box.

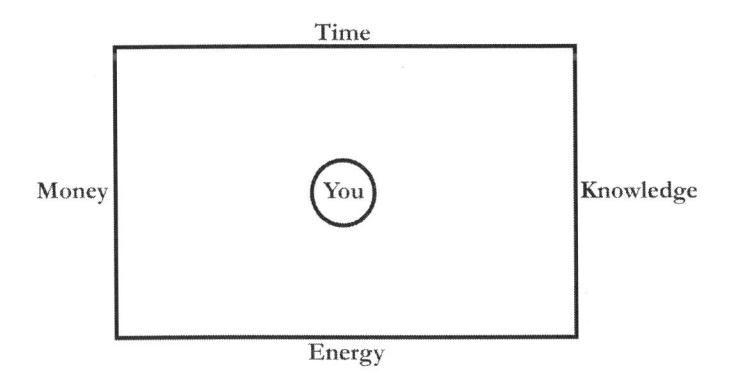

The greater your energy, the more knowledge you gain, the efficiency at which you use your time, and the money you have all dictate how big, or small, your box is. This is an example of a well-balanced, even amount of resources.

All of the empty space inside this box is the room you have for others in your life. You are the center circle, and the people in your life are represented by the other circles.

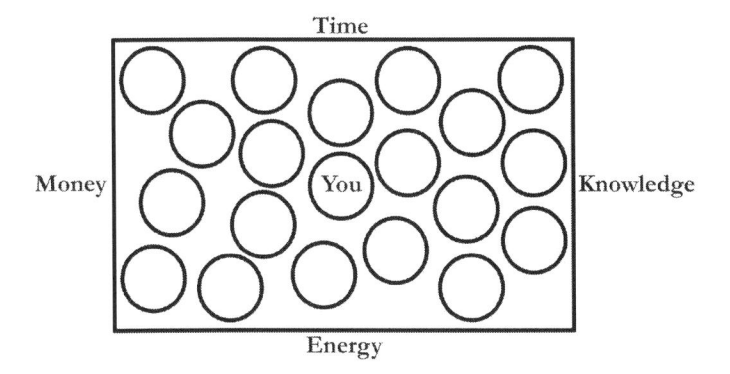

Now, this does not represent *everybody* you know. Who this represents are the people you spend *most* of your time with. Inside this box are your coworkers, your close friends, family members you see often, etc.

These are the people that you interact with the most, by choice or not. The people closest to you in this box influence you the most. These people are spouses, children, direct colleagues, and the people you choose to spend the most time with.

Something that is true in life, whether we like to admit it or not, is judgement. But not all judgement is bad. In this case, we'll actually call it an "assessment." When you assess those inside your box, you can give each of them a number. 10's are high-quality people, people with goals, people with ambitions, people that, when they're around, they lift you up! These people are energizing. You know people like this, and are likely able to think of some of them right now. What about these people is it that makes them 10's?

Next, you have the 1's. These people aren't going anywhere, they aren't involved in much of anything worthwhile, and they never have a solution to a problem. These people are draining. You can probably think of a few of them as well. Finally, there is everybody in between.

This assessment isn't PC enough for some people, I realize that. But, #sorrynotsorry. It's the truth. We assess people every day.

Theory of Resources

Your box may look something like this:

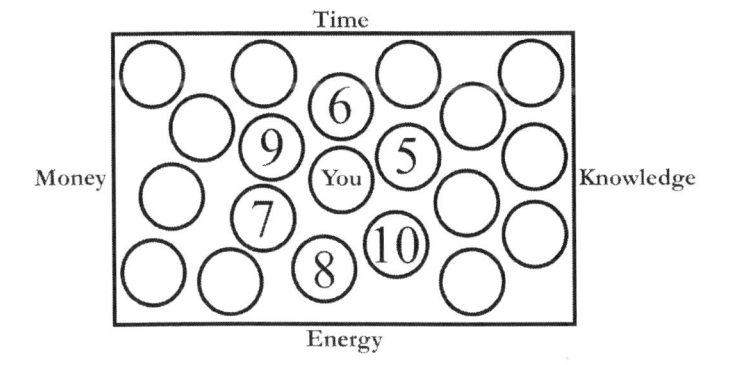

[Diagram: A box labeled with Time (top), Money (left), Knowledge (right), Energy (bottom). Inside are circles, some numbered 5, 6, 7, 8, 9, 10 around a center circle labeled "You".]

As you assess your situation, maybe you find that you have some great people immediately around you, and you also find that you have one or two people that could work on themselves a bit. The ones closest to you in the box are your influencers. These people affect you the most. Then you have everybody else in your box. Again, this isn't everybody you know, this is just everybody that actually plays an active role in your life.

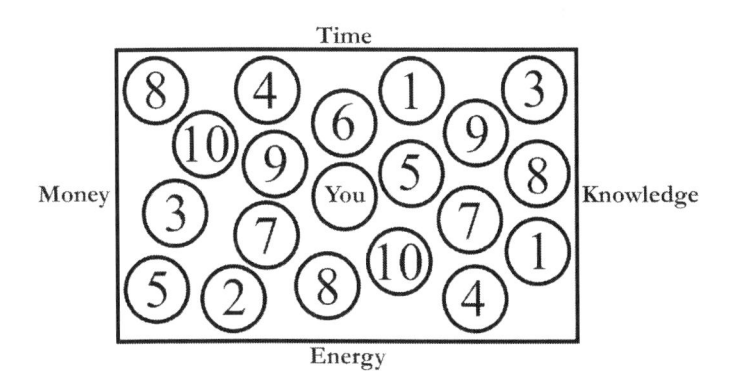

[Diagram: A box labeled with Time (top), Money (left), Knowledge (right), Energy (bottom). Inside are many numbered circles around a center "You" circle: 8, 4, 1, 3, 10, 6, 9, 5, 9, 8, 3, 7, 7, 1, 5, 2, 8, 10, 4.]

93

So here we have an example of you and your box. There is you plus 19 people who regularly impact your life. The people closer to you in the box are people who you are around more than those near the outer limits, but everybody has an effect.

Keep in mind that we said this is an evenly distributed box of resources. This is an example of a fair amount of time, energy, knowledge, and money. However, as you assess your situation, it is imperative to critically think about how much of each you actually have. Where do you excel? Where do you fall short? What could you change now to improve any one of these four? What is going to take some time to improve? These questions can help you decide what your next action steps are, but for now, I need to make sure we have a basic understanding of this box.

Consider you have a lot of knowledge, enough energy, and the right amount of money, but your time is cut short. Then your box gets shifted to something closer to this:

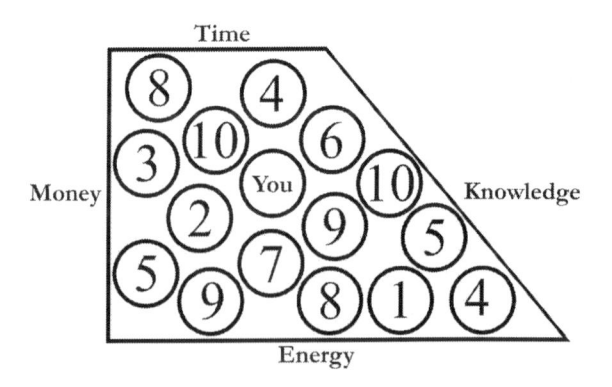

In cases like this, now you don't have as much space in your life for as many people. The number of people dropped from 19 to 15. So those you *do* spend time with, have an even greater effect on you. You can imagine how this box shifts and changes for each individual. Given we all have different measures of these resources, if you look at 10 people's boxes, you'll see 10 different shapes.

When I showed this to a friend of mine, he disagreed with the time resource. He said, "That's wrong. Everybody has 24 hours in a day." He is correct in saying that, but this measure of time is not the hours in a day. It's *how we use* those hours. Some people are so efficient they free up time for themselves. Some people use their time so poorly, it's a wonder they ever get anything done.

We all have our own box, and all of our individual boxes are different shapes, sizes, and have various distributions of these resources. With this understanding, let's dig deeper into our boxes to see if we could benefit from shifting some things around. Understanding and implementing the use of the Theory of Resources is a valuable tool for helping us identify where our beneficial and detrimental relationships are.

(Key Takeaways from chapters 14 and 15 will be grouped together at the end of chapter 15)

15
Inside The Box

Nothing makes you more vulnerable than your refusal to be honest with yourself.
– Charly Emery

Now that you have a good understanding of the Theory of Resources, it's time to do some homework. Sorry, I'm a teacher. Did you really think there wouldn't be some type of work involved in this book? The good news is that we're going to do this together.

This is the moment that, if we were in class, we'd anxiously look at each other. And we'd keep randomly glancing at one another because the teacher just said we could work in partners. Whenever my teachers would mention partner work, I'd quickly sit up, lean forward, one leg would start to bounce, and I would anxiously anticipate the teacher's instruction to arrange our desks. For some reason, I always felt like if I didn't keep an eye on my partner, they might vanish. Anyway, pardon my random memory.

I mean for this to be a mental exercise, but if you'd like to write it down, it definitely wouldn't hurt. Think about the four resources. Think about what your box looks like. Which of the four do you have the most of? What do you need more of? What are you doing that limits each resource? Could you adjust anything in your life to change (read: improve) the shape of your box? Getting an idea of where you are in terms of each resource is a great starting place. Without knowing what we currently have at our disposal, we can't accurately assess anything. Stay with me, we're about to get to the really good stuff.

Your box has a shape. For the sake of this discussion, I am going to use this example box.

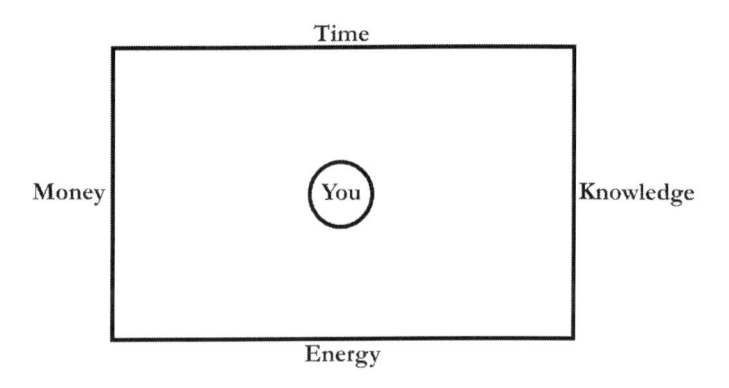

```
              Time

Money         You         Knowledge

             Energy
```

Next, think about the 4-6 people you spend the most time with and answer three questions.

- Who are they?
- Is spending so much time with them a choice?
- What *honest* rating would you give each of them?

These people are likely going to be a significant other, coworkers, children (if you have them), or close friends. Most of the time, we don't really have the option of not being around these people. As for the assessment, *be critically honest*. There is no point in taking a snapshot of your life if you're just going to put an unrealistic filter on it anyway.

- What are these people working toward?
- How do these people treat you?
- How do these people treat other people?
- Do they keep their word?
- Are they more likely to compliment you or criticize you?

I use these questions because they force an honest assessment of those around us without giving us the opportunity to give somebody an out. What I mean is that sometimes we afford people slack when we shouldn't, because it's easier to make an excuse for somebody rather than inviting them to make a change. This type of thinking only hurts us. Take a moment, really think through this part. But before we populate this box, there is one more variable I want to add that I didn't mention in the previous chapter.

This is going to change how the circles look a little bit. We know that each circle represents a person. And in my prior examples, every circle was the same size. However, some people are much more influential than others. For example, one of the people I'm around might be a coworker I see daily, but they really don't affect me too much. This person's circle won't be very big. Conversely, I might have a coworker who is very impactful on me, positively or negatively, their circle is going to be larger. So, with your 4-6 people closest to you, your box will look something like this:

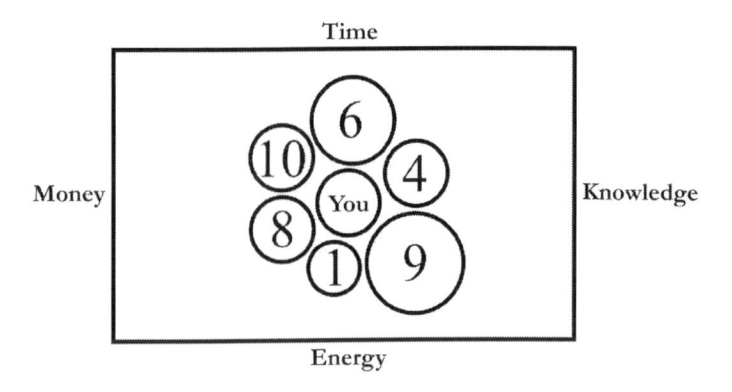

Diagram: Influence Box Example

```
                    Time
    ┌─────────────────────────────────────┐
    │              ( 6 )                  │
    │         (10)(You)( 4 )              │
Money│          ( 8 )                     │Knowledge
    │           ( 1 )( 9 )                │
    └─────────────────────────────────────┘
                   Energy
```

You see in this example a very influential 9 and 6, a quality 10 and 8 who are somewhat impactful, and a 4 and 1. What does your box look like? Matter of fact, I give you permission to write in the book.

In the following box, fill in the 4-6 people you spend the *most* time with, adjust the size of their circle according to their influence on you, and then write in a number. (Word of advice: if the rating is low, don't write a name next to it. No need for a senseless argument if they ever happen to see it) ☺

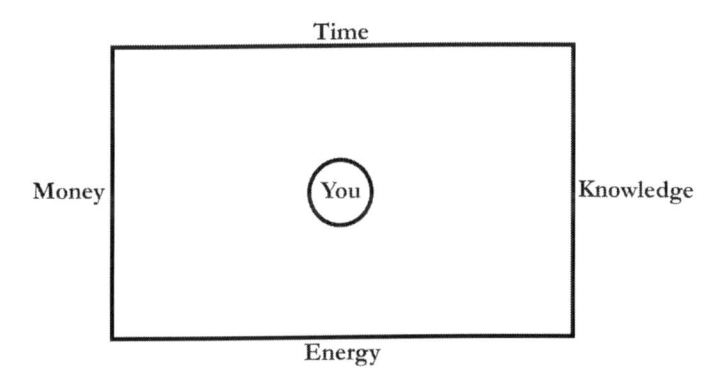

```
                    Time
    ┌─────────────────────────────────────┐
    │                                     │
    │                                     │
Money│            ( You )                 │Knowledge
    │                                     │
    │                                     │
    └─────────────────────────────────────┘
                   Energy
```

Critical question: are you genuinely happy with those around you who are the most impactful? Are you regularly rubbing shoulders with 8's, 9's, and 10's? Or are you putting up with sub-5's? It's not always easy to be honest, but it's important that you are because *this is your life*.

If you are surrounded by people who are bringing you down, one of two things *must* happen if you are to turn it around and live a satisfied life.

1- They have to improve.
2- You have to limit your exposure to them.

Changing the 4-6 people who are closest to you is not a quick and easy process. In some cases, the people on the outer edge of your box are a bit easier to shuffle around, but those close to you are a different story.

I realize that this sounds like I am talking about people like they're pawns in your game of life. But you have to understand this: if you are not proactive in creating your ideal life, with your ideal relationships, then you're passively leaving the quality of your life up to a by-product chance of other people's decisions. I have to make sure you didn't miss that.

If you are not proactive in creating your ideal life, with your ideal relationships, then you're passively leaving the quality of your life up to a by-product chance of other people's decisions.

Is that all you deserve?

Key Takeaways from Chapters 14 & 15

1- We have a limited amount of resources which limit us to what we can do and who we can associate ourselves with. We must utilize our time and relationships to the best of our ability.

2- Assess the people around you. Are they lifting you up or taking you down?

3- Change what you can change. You must be proactive in choosing who you are around. Your environment plays a major role in your success and your level of satisfaction.

16
Quitting To Start

"Coulda, woulda, shoulda" are the last words of a fool.
– Tobe Nwigwe

The summer after I graduated college in 2012, I went and completed an audit internship for an accounting firm in Boise, Idaho. I was excited for the internship because it was a change of pace from the monotony of school work that was comprised of balance sheets and accounting theories. My pay was literally doubling from a different internship I took at the university during the semester, I wasn't going to have "homework," and I was moving from a city of 50,000 people to a city of 500,000. It was the perfect formula.

I quickly got settled into Boise thanks to some close friends who were generous enough to let me stay with them for the summer. My box of resources looked different in Boise. I knew fewer people, but they were all quality individuals. I can safely say that I don't feel like I was surrounded by anybody less than a 7 or 8. I was in a great internship, working for a solid firm, surrounded by hard-working, fun professionals (contrary to popular belief, accountants are actually legally allowed to have fun), and I was making better money than I could have at any job on campus. However, as quickly as I got settled, the excitement of my new situation wore off. The day-in and day-out work of an auditor got old, and it got old quickly.

I didn't love accounting. I slipped into studying it from secondary education because of an interest in finance, but then was talked into accounting by a professor who all but told me that an accounting degree is everything a finance degree could dream of, plus a career of attractive compensation. Whether true or not, I found that I wasn't absolutely loving the audit internship. Don't get me wrong, I wasn't *miserable*, but I also wasn't waking up in the morning eager to reference a company's documents to what their ledgers portrayed. I thought that maybe it was because I was an intern and was just possibly doing the not-so-fun stuff. *"Once I get my CPA license,"* I told myself, *"then I'll be happy."*

The summer internship ended and I started the Masters of Accountancy (MAcc) program at Idaho State University. I had pretty much begged my friend Matt, who had also recently received his accounting degree, to do it with me. I told him we could pass the CPA exam together. He agreed.

Well, one month into the program I realized that nothing was going to change for me and my relationship with accounting. I just wasn't loving it. I had completed two accounting internships with amazing people, I was in the MAcc program with amazing people, but I felt *far* from amazing. I loathed my daily schedule.

Finally, the semester ended and it couldn't have happened soon enough. I had been pretty out-spoken to my wife (we were dating then) about how much I didn't like the program. I felt unsatisfied. It was the same feeling I had doing audits, the only difference now was that I was back in an academic setting. She told me that she supported whatever decision I would make. She played a major role in helping me decide to not continue pursuing the MAcc, and instead I did taxes and worked as a substitute teacher during the spring.

I want to point something out that is extremely important to recognize. At my internship, I had everything I needed to be happy. I was living in an active city, being compensated better than I had been before, and was surrounded by great people. So what was the problem? What could I possibly have complained about? Why did I feel dull, uninspired? *This* is what I realized:

> My day-to-day responsibilities and my day-to-day accomplishments were not things that I *truly* cared about. They were things that I had been pursuing because I let an idea of security and income catch my attention. But security and income do nothing for you if you're not actively engaged in pursuing the things you're passionate about. They are merely sufficient distractions, at best.

Mentally, it wasn't an easy transition. I felt responsible for Matt's involvement in the program and now I had to tell him I wasn't continuing. Good thing "we're friends because we're both really awesome and better than everybody else," right?

In addition to that, I had to convince myself that making this choice was the right one even though pursuing teaching (what I originally wanted to do) meant I was going to make substantially less money. But like I said, security and income mean nothing if we don't pursue what we are passionate about.

My first day in the classroom as a substitute teacher confirmed

The Golden Connection

every thought I had. I was in the right place. My days were full, I was having fun, and I felt like I was utilizing my skillset in an arena that benefited from it. Please do not read this as me talking down on accountants, or their work. Their purpose is necessary and their contributions are great, it's just that it wasn't for me.

So, during the spring of 2013, I did taxes part-time and was a part-time substitute teacher while I started the necessary process to get my teaching certificate. I wasn't going to be able to be a full-time teacher at least until the coming fall, so I had to keep myself productive during the summer. That's when I spent three months with somebody who endured more in his first 10 years of being born than most people do in a lifetime.

At 7 years old, doctors found a tumor on Caden Pickett's brain. Within a year, he had a shunt that releases pressure caused by the tumor. To date, he has had more than 70 brain surgeries. S-E-V-E-N-T-Y. 70! Try, just for a second, to fathom that. In a decade of life, he has undergone an average of one brain surgery every other month.

Caden and I spent the summer of 2013 together. I worked with him doing psycho-social rehab. That's a fancy way of saying we spent time working on self-improvement, being an active, contributing member of society, and decision-making skills. Since being introduced to the idea that we can better ourselves if we try, I knew Caden's determination would allow him to stretch himself beyond what he currently thought. Anybody who has lasted through one brain surgery is an incredible fighter, let alone 70+!

We spent the summer working on goal-setting, reading his first personal development book, and introduced him to being physically active through weight-training. I believe there to be a strong positive correlation between a healthy body and a healthy mind. If your body isn't feeling right, your mind can't quite feel right.

It was a bit of a process to get into our routine as Caden wasn't immediately fond of reading. We would take turns reading *The Anatomy of Peace* out loud, but when it was his turn to read, he'd usually start trying to sell me on the idea of running to a nearby gas station to pick up a cold Monster energy drink or go and get some food. But, we eventually did get into the routine of read, workout, hangout, read, workout, hangout.

Before I started working with Caden, I had toyed with the idea of a different summer job that would pay more. With my wife and I getting married and a move halfway across the country coming up in the fall, the prospect of more money was attractive, but ultimately I knew that I wanted to be actively engaged in something, or someone, I thought was worthwhile. I think of that summer as a microcosm of what my life might be like: choose money over purpose, or realize that I have one life to live so I better spend it doing something I believe in.

Sometimes I really questioned my decision, though. One day we were at the gym and I was showing Caden a new workout. It involved a declined bench that he was lying on while simultaneously throwing me a medicine ball. With each time he would sit up, he would toss me the medicine ball, then I'd return it on his way back down. One time, he thought it would be funny (typically not a good start to any sentence) to not just "toss" the ball back to me, but see if he could get the ball through my hands. He succeeded. My hands acted like curtains in the wind and the ball made its way to my face. I immediately thought, *This is it. I am actually going to kill him.* Well, I didn't, but I was so mad. What made it worse is Caden could not stop laughing!

> Picture this: two guys in the gym, one gets hit in the face with a medicine ball by the other, the aggressor can't stop laughing hysterically while the other tries reprimanding him, but with each reprimand, the laughs only become more intense and uncontrollable. Right in that moment, I asked myself why I had chosen to do this instead of working elsewhere.

Well, the feelings of doubt quickly subsided, and we went about the rest of our routine. There were moments like this one littered throughout the summer, but that's what kept it fun.

Needless to say, that summer was not a waste. Caden might tell you that he learned a thing or two from me, but not nearly as much as I learned from him. His resilience, his ability to laugh at life, and his willingness to learn new things kept each day fresh.

I bring this up to compare the two summers I had experienced. The former summer I had everything you could ask for, on paper. The latter summer I had chosen to do something I saw personal value in rather than security or a paycheck.

When you pursue things to make somebody else happy, simply to make more money, or because you think it's what you're *supposed* to do, you cheat yourself of finding the purpose of each day. You cheat yourself and those around you of the best, happiest version of you.

The summer with Caden wasn't all rainbows and unicorns, but this is what it showed me:

> When we focus on being involved in what we believe to

be our purpose, there is no way you can't feel productive. There is no way to *not* be satisfied with your work. And that's the problem with a majority of people who are unhappy. They are unhappy because they are involved in day-to-day work that they don't really find value in. People get stuck in ruts and are too afraid to make a move because of security, or sometimes it's just inertia, but for whatever reason, they stay.

I know teachers who would probably be happier and more effective as accountants, and I know some accountants who would thrive in the world of education. But, we allow ourselves and our lives to be dictated by dogma, by the influence of others, or by the belief that "I've invested too much time already" to make a change.

In short, be you. Only when you are *you*, can you really help them be *them*!

Now I want to get back to the box. How do the rest of the people affect us? What if we are surrounded by people who are bringing us down? Before we get into this, let me say that there is a reason we call them growing *pains*. Growth is rarely easy, often uncomfortable, and sometimes painful.

THE Key Takeaway from Chapter 16

1- Pursuing a paycheck leaves you feeling discontent. Pursuing your passion leaves you feeling fulfilled.

17
You Can't Stay Dry In A Pool

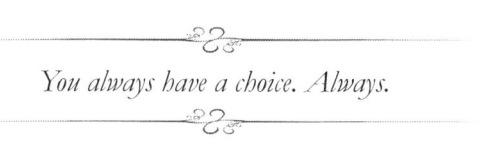

You always have a choice. Always.

There are good relationships and bad relationships. That much is obvious. But why do we deal with bad relationships for as long as we do? Why do we hold on to things that make us feel drained at best and miserable at worst? Are we forced to interact with the pessimists, the nay-sayers, and the complainers? What if the 1's, 2's, and 3's aren't really people you can just cut out of your life? To answer these questions, I need you to come on a mental journey with me. It will better help illustrate what I am saying.

Imagine a young boy standing in front of you. He is about half your height, and he is looking up at you. His eyes are watery, his expression glum, and his clothes are soaking wet. The sun is setting and there is a slight breeze causing the boy to shiver. He is complaining that he is cold. He turns, and starts to walk away.

You follow him close enough to not lose sight of him, but far enough away that he doesn't notice you. After a while, you see him enter into the fenced backyard of a home where you see him walk up to a small, one-foot tall, blue, plastic kiddie pool that is full of water. He stands looking at the pool inquisitively. You see a pillow floating in the water.

With the sun completely gone now, the breeze constant, the boy steps into the pool, lies down with his head on the pillow, and goes to sleep. You watch, speechless, as the boy tosses and turns from the obvious discomfort of the pool. On his side, to his back, to his other side, the boy fights the wet and cold as he tries to rest. You see his natural response of his cold hands vigilantly trying to rub warmth into his cold arms. You have no words as you're left standing there shaking your head. You watch miniature ripples dance across the surface of the water from the easy breeze.

The next evening, this same boy approaches you and complains he is still soaking wet, still cold. You look pitifully at him, fully understanding why he is wet and cold. You try to tell him what's wrong, but before you can get any words out, he turns and walks away. Again, you follow him, watching his water-logged clothing wave in the soft breeze.

You stare, dumbstruck, as you watch him approach the same backyard, and climb into the same plastic pool. He sleeps, restlessly. He doesn't seem to see it, but you know what he needs to change. You know why he is cold, wet, and constantly shivering.

The next day, you approach the boy and tell him that he can't

You Can't Stay Dry In A Pool

keep getting into the pool. He shoots an angry look at you and says, "The only way I can get away from the cold breeze is by getting in the water! It's colder *outside* of the pool than it is *inside* of the pool!"

"But your clothes are soaking wet *because* of the pool." You say, sharply.

He looks down and shakes his head, "You don't get it, I can't stand the cold! The breeze is too much to deal with, that's why I have to get back into the pool!"

"But if you stay *out* of the pool…"

He interrupts, "I can't feel the breeze in the pool!"

"You can't stay dry in a pool!" You fire back.

The conversation hits a wall of silence. He looks at you, blinking a drop of water off of his eyelash. Finally, he says the only thing he feels he can say, "You just don't understand." He turns and walks away, his shoes making a squishy watery sound with each step. All you can do is shake your head in bewilderment.

You know this little boy. Matter of fact, we all know this little boy. And, for some of you reading this, you *are* that little boy. In this story, the pool full of water represents unfavorable relationships. As we imagined our way through the story, we saw the boy standing right next to the pool, looking at it as if he was evaluating whether or not he wanted to get in. As he weighed what seemed to be only two options, he made a conscious decision to get into the pool so he could escape the breeze.

The problems people face today are very similar to this boy's dilemma. People are making conscious decisions to *stay* in a bad place. People are making conscious decisions to *not* improve their situations. Whether it's a job problem, a money problem, a health problem, or a relationship problem, people are literally *choosing* to stay where they are.

The most frustrating part of this all is that they don't see what is right in front of their eyes. They blame everything around them. They blame the breeze, they blame the water, they blame the wet clothes, they blame a bad night of sleep, and they blame the sun going down like it's the sun's fault that it goes down causing night to come! But what they'll never blame is *their own deliberate actions* that put them where they are.

Furthermore, when we try to shed light on somebody's problems, they don't want to, or they cannot see it. They don't want to hear that *they* are the ones choosing not to change their situation. Not only do they not want to hear it, they get defensive about it! So it is with poor relationships. People are sometimes making the choice to stay exposed to toxic environments.

One truth that we face as human beings is having to deal with crabby people every now and then. We can't rid the entire world of crabby people, but we can rid *our* world of crabby people. By choosing to interact with these people we are choosing to limit our happiness and our progress. Just as the little boy had the opportunity to not get into the pool, we usually have the opportunity to not engage in poor relationships.

I shared this idea with my students one day in class. A girl raised her hand and asked, "What if your *mom* is the crabby person?" The class laughed, and I couldn't help but join them, because she had a fair question. In some cases, the 1, 2, or 3 isn't somebody you can just cut ties with and never look back. Sometimes these people are family members or close friends that can't practically be avoided. However, we still have the choice of how much we're around them.

As people who value bettering ourselves, we might even consider dedicating a part of our day, week, or some amount of time to helping a 1 get to a 2, a 2 to a 3, and so on. If we can help somebody see a clearer vision, we have that responsibility. But we have to know when it's time to cut it off, because some people are so naturally negative that they aren't happy unless they're mad. It sounds funny, but it's true.

If you have ever spent a substantial amount of time with these kinds of people, you know what I am talking about. They can be draining. Spending time with 1's, 2's, and 3's limits you to a lot of things. It limits you to being productive for yourself because it seems like you're always helping them fix their problems, or getting them out of their dilemmas. It seems like there is always *something* going wrong for them. Oh, and it's never their fault. The victim mentality is strong with 1's, 2's, and 3's. You can only be around them so much until one of two things will happen:

1- You make a deliberate decision to not be exposed to their negativity anymore.
2- Their negativity eventually starts to affect your mood in an adverse way.

To clarify, they obviously aren't bad people, they simply aren't the best to be around in terms of getting things done. I not only believe that productivity promotes positivity, I believe that productivity *precedes* positivity. A lot of people aren't happy because they aren't *doing*, they aren't working towards something of value. They're the ones that we identify as the people who always need help fixing their problems because they aren't doing anything about them.

Criticisms that I have received for this idea stem from the belief that I am suggesting we only look to people who can lift us up. It might sound like I am saying "Forget anybody who doesn't have something to offer you." That is absolutely not the case. We have to be willing to help those around us, if they're willing to meet us at least halfway. If they're willing to meet us at least halfway. That wasn't a typo, it's just important enough to read it twice. It's perfectly worthwhile to spend time with a group of 2's that are working like crazy to become 3's. That's productive, that's goal-oriented, *they* are worth your time. It's when people are stagnantly existing through each day that we must have the ability to say "I can't afford to spend any more time and energy on somebody who isn't equally as ambitious for their own improvement." When you rid your life of a pessimistic 2, you make way for a productive 8, 9, or 10.

This reminds me of a famous idea that says to attract motivated people, you must be motivated. To attract genuine people, you must be genuine. At the end of the day, we all know that Eagles don't fly with pigeons and Lions don't run with hyenas. But, you can't merely *want* quality relationships, you have to *deserve* quality relationships.

Your relationships are an investment. If your box is full of people on the bottom half of the scale, if you're spending a majority of your time with a bunch of 5's or lower, you will not find satisfaction. I'll say it again, I know this sounds harsh to put a number on people, but it's only harsh because it's true. And since it's true, you better take a good look at those around you. People are an investment, and some of your investments might be costing you substantially more than you realize you're paying.

Key Takeaways from Chapter 17

1- Some of the bad circumstances we find ourselves in stem from our own poor decision making.

2- You either limit your exposure to negative people, or they'll start to influence your mindset.

3- Invest in those around you who are ready to invest in themselves. Otherwise, move on.

18
The Journey

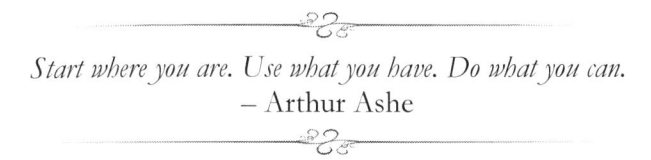

Start where you are. Use what you have. Do what you can.
– Arthur Ashe

I was at a conference when I heard a story about a man who had just landed a job in corporate America making $30,000 a year. He was ambitious, he had goals, and he knew he wanted to be at the top. He had his sights set on being the CEO.

One day in the lobby, he spots the current CEO of the company. He runs over, introduces himself, and somehow talks the CEO into a lunch meeting in the near future. Ecstatic, he picks up the phone to call his friend to tell him about what he had managed to set up.

"What do you mean 'why did I do that?'" He asked. "I saw him in the lobby so I took the opportunity to say something. Now I have a meeting with the C-E-O of the company!"

"What I mean is that CEO isn't going to help you get to where you want to be." The well-meaning friend replies.

"What are you talking about? We have a lunch meeting set up."

"That CEO isn't going to be able to tell what you need to do next. That CEO is making $500,000 a year, you're making $30,000 a year. What you need to do is set up a lunch meeting with somebody making $40,000 a year, then focus on that. Once you're there, find somebody making $50,000, and pick their brain."

Talk about a buzz kill, right? Sort of. Advice like this, though seemingly abrupt, is spot on. Now, is it a complete waste to sit down with somebody who is leaps and bounds ahead of you in terms of skillset/career? No. Not necessarily. But what he was trying to teach is that, if you're on level 2, try to get to level 3 instead of focusing on level 20.

In this book we have covered the importance of attempting something difficult, taking lessons from hardships, the benefits of relationships, the significance of transparency, the value of assessing those around us, and much more. But we can't do everything all the time.

Much like the entry-level worker in a corporation, rather than trying to get to CEO in a week, we have to focus on one or two specific areas to improve in. When we consistently work on ourselves, we see progress. When we see progress we're motivated. When we're motivated, we see even *more* results. When we witness great results, it keeps the cycle going.

I recently read Greg E. Hill's Book titled *Remember You're A Genius Again*, in which he discusses many of his experiences and setbacks. He talks about his ups, downs, and everything in between. He tells about his experience starting his own business, making a lot of money, but then later finding himself broke and suicidal. It got me thinking that if you look at him today, you might say he was born great. But his struggles have taught him lessons that he has had to apply to his life to get him to a better place now than where he was before.

I know you can think of athletes, entrepreneurs, and people in every other industry who have had to struggle their way to the top. From Charles Darwin to Walt Disney and countless others in-between, individuals have overcome enormous setbacks, criticisms, and defeats. Yet, they continued moving forward, one step at a time, and have become massively influential in their respective arenas.

One of my favorite stories of persistence and improvement is about Stephen King's novel *Carrie*. It's reported that he was so unimpressed and frustrated with it that he finally ended up throwing it in the garbage. He literally, threw it all away. His wife happened to find it in the trashcan while he was out of the house. She opened the crinkled papers, read it, and thought it was worth working on. Stephen King, the genius writer, didn't believe in it, but his wife did. Long story short, it did take off. The finished product was still rejected dozens and dozens of times, but eventually he received a "yes" in the form of the biggest check he had been given to date.

Using this story is perfectly fitting for *The Golden Connection*. Stephen King had within him all the necessary tools to write a masterpiece. He just had to keep at it and not give up. When the pushback and struggles of being a writer became too big, he tried to say *"forget it!"* But, his wife wouldn't let him. In our own lives, sometimes we have to struggle, work, struggle, work, struggle, work and it still feels like we come up short. That's why the relationships around us are so critical. When we struggle to see our own greatness, our support system is there to remind us that we're capable. We can't expect solid support from suspect relationships. We *must* do our best to surround ourselves with people that are striving for more.

I'll bet that Stephen King didn't anticipate *Carrie* being a source of inspiration for people, but like most things in life, there is a positive lesson in everything. Becoming a household name is not the standard for somebody to be deemed a success, constant effort and improvement is.

Improvement isn't easy, progress isn't convenient, but success isn't for everybody. I believe everybody has what it takes to find it, but not everybody is willing to go through the journey of it all to get there.

One of my favorite songs is called "Ten Thousand Hours" by the artist Macklemore. Author/Speaker Malcolm Gladwell argues that 10,000 hours is the amount of focused practice that it takes to master something. In Macklemore's song, he dropped more truth in a few lines than some musicians do in their entire careers:

> *See, I observed Escher. I love Basquiat.*
> *I watched Keith Haring. You see I study art.*
> *The greats weren't great because at birth they could paint,*
> *the greats were great because they paint a lot.*

I can't imagine how many pieces M.C. Escher, Jean-Michel Basquiat, and Keith Haring (along with countless other artists) have thrown away. In the same way that an artist has to adjust, refine, and redo their work, we are the artists of our own lives who must constantly adjust, refine, and redo ourselves. That's not to say we're not good enough. Quite the contrary, actually. We're so incredible that it would be a waste for us to *not* look for those ways to improve.

There is one last piece we must consider in the journey of building our relationships, including the one we have with ourselves. Just know that you *will* mess up. You will make mistakes, sometimes big ones. Maybe even *terrible* ones. You have to keep moving forward. Growth is a journey.

In over three decades of life, I still have *a lot* to learn. We all do. The mistakes in our past prove that to be true. But what those mistakes also prove is there is an opportunity for us to get better. Our blemishes, bumps, bruises, and rough edges are what make us relatable to others. They're the experiences that allow you to reach others when they're broken. They're the tools you can use to look somebody in their sorrowful eyes and say "I've been where you are, I've hurt how you're hurting, and I've cried how you're crying." Don't be ashamed of your failures, be empowered by them.

So, what exactly is The Golden Connection? When it's all said and done, it's really the relationship you have with yourself and those around you. If you are who you portray yourself to be, if you strive to be a better person daily, and if you can learn from your mistakes while having hope in the future, you've discovered what The Golden Connection is. Nothing is more empowering than being the genuine you. When you become this person, you position yourself to be a force for change, an advocate for good, and an example to those around you.

I whole-heartedly believe we all have something to offer. If anybody makes you feel differently, that's an issue *they* need to work out, not you. Keep being you, keep being incredible, and don't ever forget…

MOVE FORWARD. MAKE A DIFFERENCE. BE A FACTOR.

Connect With Me

@goljali

I would love it if you shared with me something you got from reading this book. Find me on Facebook, Twitter, Instagram, or Snapchat.

www.aligoljahmofrad.com

Keep being you.

Made in the USA
Columbia, SC
10 August 2019